D0847725

BookMarks

BookMarks

Reading in Black and White

A memoir by

KARLA FC HOLLOWAY

Rutgers University Press

New Brunswick, New Jersey, and London

Library of Congress Cataloging-in-Publication Data

Holloway, Karla F. C., 1949–

   BookMarks : reading in Black and white : a memoir / by Karla FC Holloway.

      p. cm.

   Includes bibliographical references (p.) and index.

   ISBN-13: 978-0-8135-3907-2 (alk. paper)

   1. African Americans—Books and reading.   2. American literature—African American authors—
History and criticism.   3. African Americans in literature.   4. African Americans and libraries.
5. African Americans—Intellectual life.   I. Title.

   Z1039.B56H65 2006

   028′.908996073 — dc22

                                                                                              2006005585

A British Cataloging-in-Publication record for this book is available from the British Library.

Text design by Karolina Harris

Manufactured in the United States of America

for Leslie

and for

Maxwell, Miles, and Zoë Andrea

Contents

Acknowledgments   ix

Prologue—A Reader's Place   1

1. Reading and Desire in a Room of Their Own   13
   The booklists of JESSIE FAUSET and MARITA GOLDEN

2. A Negro Library   27
   The booklists of W.E.B. DU BOIS, RALPH ELLISON,
   and RICHARD WRIGHT

3. On Censorship and Tarzan   55
   The booklists of JOHN HOPE FRANKLIN, SONIA SANCHEZ,
   and AUDRE LORDE

4. A Prison Library   75
   The booklists of ANGELA DAVIS, MALCOLM X,
   and ELDRIDGE CLEAVER

5. The Anchor Bar   91
   The booklists of MAYA ANGELOU and JAMES BALDWIN

6. A Proud Chestnut   105
   The booklists of JAMES WELDON JOHNSON
   and NIKKI GIOVANNI

7. The Children's Room   117
   The booklists of LANGSTON HUGHES and PAULI MURRAY

8. My Mother's Singing   131
   The booklists of C. ERIC LINCOLN and LEON FORREST

9. Reading Race   143
   The booklists of HENRY LOUIS GATES and MICHAEL
   ERIC DYSON

10. The Card Catalog   167
    The booklists of ZORA NEALE HURSTON, J. SAUNDERS
    REDDING, OCTAVIA BUTLER, SAMUEL DELANEY,
    and OPRAH WINFREY

Epilogue—Pondering Color   191

Author Profiles   195
Notes   207
Sources   211
Index   215

Acknowledgments

I COMPLETED *BookMarks* in the idyllic and storied landscapes of the villas Serbelloni and Maranese in Bellagio, Italy. My sincere thanks to the Rockefeller Foundation for the gift of that fellowship and its extraordinary company. The staff and administration of the villas, especially Pilar Palacia, have my thanks for sustaining so wonderfully that magical space for its residents.

Over the years of this manuscript, several persons have provided editorial and research assistance. I am indebted to Evelyn Shockley, Stephane Robolin, Allison Puckett, Amy Williams, and Kendrea Tannis for their invaluable research support and their careful and attentive responses to my requests and for their generous contributions of imagination and time. My special thanks and gratitude go to Erin Gentry, whose persistent, interested, and intelligent research during one summer considerably eased the process of publication and made this a better book, and Kathryn Gohl for her expert and thoughtful editorial advice. Rudolph P. Byrd, himself ensconced in that magical Bellagio moment, listened and responded with encouragement and interest as he shared insights that were invaluable in my consideration of James Weldon Johnson. He added symmetry, grace, intelligence, and good humor to those autumnal days. My colleagues William Chafe, Deborah McDowell, and Henry Louis Gates Jr. gave crucial support when this manuscript was in its earliest stages. I acknowledge as well—and with thanks—their friendship, thoughtful interest, and kind attention, which have been, for many more years than this manuscript's existence, consistent and generous. Libraries have been especially important to this book's generation and its completion. In my research and recall of the libraries that have mattered so much to this book, their help was invaluable and generous. The reference librarians at Duke University's Perkins Library received questions and offered help with gracious and professional goodwill and interest. My thanks as well to the reference librarian Laura Schiefer at the Buffalo and Erie County Historical Society for her rapid and enthusiastic response to my late-day query about a photograph. The librarians at Talladega College's Savery Library, Juliette Smith and Asma Alwan, made me remember why it was such a special place, and I am grateful to them for nurturing so well the legacy of that historic place. Leslie Mitchner, my editor at Rutgers, read the outsides and insides of the manuscript, knew intuitively and well its lacunae, encouraged the evolution of the final project, and read drafts and redrafts with deliberation and thoughtfulness. I am fortunate to have benefited from her generous friendship and dedicated professionalism over many years. Ayana and Russell were always at and on my side, always heart-near, and always embracing the center of this story as they do my every day. They share that space with those who lovingly haunt my memories—Ouida Eleanor, Claude D'Arcy, Karen Andrea, Paschal Michael Chigozie, and Bem Kayin. But it is my mother, Ouida, who shaped my love of books and their places and whose own fierce model of intelligence, wisdom, and loving-kindness slips into these pages.

BookMarks is dedicated, with love, to my sister Leslie Ellen and with confidence and devotion to Zoë, Max, and Miles, because although our generations shift and change, we are all fully embraced within the sturdy legacies of these stories and their telling.

BookMarks

I've always felt that the stories we tell ourselves about the books which we only know slightly and fleetingly, by rumor or inflationary report, end up being even more "influential" than the works we encounter full on, absorb, judge and come to occupy some balanced relation with. From those books we absorb the unquestioned laws of genre . . . conventional attitudes and expectations. From the others, however, we manufacture the dream of possibility, of variation, of what might be done outside and beyond.

SAMUEL DELANY, *The Motion of Light in Water*

Prologue

A Reader's Place

Make me. Remake me. You are free to do it and I am free to let you because look, look. Look where your hands are. Now.

TONI MORRISON, *Jazz*

IT would seem that too many years have passed between this event and this telling for me to remember it at all. It may be a lingering guilt that encourages it to hover, securing it to my memory, even though I suspect it has gained more significance than necessary. My father always said I was too hard on myself. But his expectations and standards are actually a part of this story—because if it were not for his dedicated interest in assuring that his daughters would always be a credit to the race, I might not have taken my seventh-grade English teacher's assignment so seriously. But it was not only my father who motivated my conduct. It was also my sister.

As a new seventh grader in the year-old Millard Fillmore Junior High School, I had an advantage. My older sister Karen had been there the year before, and she gave me all the information I needed to know not to make a fool of myself during my first year. Hers was obviously self-serving advice, given that the worst thing that could happen was that I might do something to embarrass her. Nevertheless, I was grateful for the counsel. So when I was assigned the same English teacher she had had the year before, who was also the coolest teacher in the school—Victor Lama—Karen told me how lucky I was and not to blow it.

Victor Lama was a legend in the honors English classes. He was a small man with reddish blond hair that was clearly thinning. But his reputation for being classy and smart, if not a bit iconoclastic, made him the teacher of choice. He paced between our desks and the back of the classroom and lectured from any and all spaces of the room, but he was most at home at the front of the classroom near the chalkboard. His favorite classes would earn his whimsical drawings of two figures he called Abercrombie and Minerva. He might turn to sketch one of these caricatures and place savvy quips over their heads, with comic-strip-character speech balloons that would give the next day's assignment or hint at a joke known only to that class. As a matter of fact, these drawings were only heads themselves, with two stick legs holding up giant faces that today have a bit too much in common with the popular yellow "smiley" face for me to pass by any of these without remembering that English class. But the bottom line was that Victor Lama was undoubtedly the teacher to impress, and I wanted to be deserving. For his first assignment he put a blank 3 × 5 card on our desks and asked us to list the magazines that we read in our homes.

I looked at the card and knew my fate lay in that rectangle. His judgment of me was to be fully constructed there, and I had the chance of a seventh-grade lifetime to make him know how smart I was and how cool as well.

I don't believe it ever occurred to me to list magazines that were not in our home—given the separation of years from this event, it's possible. But I was also a rather cautious adolescent, and although I was easily given to a certain amount of poetic license, it would have been uncharacteristic of me to engage in a total fiction. So I'm fairly certain I stuck to the magazines that actually did come to our home on Hughes Avenue. I do, however, remember quite clearly the thinking that went into each of my selections.

Time was a safe bet so it went to the head of the list—knowing about the world was important. My geography class (we still had geography then) made that apparent. But then there was the matter of the monthly *National Geographic* that made its way into our mailbox. That magazine dared to photograph people as objects, and the people often looked like me without my clothes on. Did I want him to associate those naked women with me? Did I want him to flip through the pages of that magazine to see why I might have listed it and then to confront a bare-breasted brown-skinned African girl and think of me? No way. It was seventh grade. I was having enough difficulty getting used to the changes in my body by myself. I did not need my English teacher's participation. *National Geographic* did not make the list. But I knew I needed a smart magazine, so the *Scientific American* that came reliably and sat just as reliably on a coffee table until replaced by the newest issue made the list. That looks good, I must have thought. *Time* and *Scientific American*. But then I needed something more credible. It was a choice between *Ebony* and *Reader's Digest*. I chose *Ebony*. If there were going to be some association between text and body in the mind of my English teacher (why else would he have asked us for this list?) why not implant the upwardly mobile, impeccably dressed and pressed black folk who had been selected for the pictorials of *Ebony* into his head. Plus, their homes were showcased in the magazine, and these homes looked as if they came from dreamland. Unlike my black teachers, who were members of our community, he would have no idea where I lived—or at least, what the inside of our home looked like. This was a chance to indicate to him that there were some black folk in America who lived in palatial splendor—at least in *Ebony* magazine. He might even think I knew some of these people. And the idea that he might associate me with those who lived in the magnificent homes pictured in *Ebony* made the choice between *Ebony* and *Reader's Digest* really no contest. But that was a pretty short list. So I lengthened it by adding my father's fraternity journal. The Greek letters in its name were prominently displayed across the top of the magazine and could certainly be impressive. Would he think I knew Greek? Why not take the chance that he might? He would see that I knew at least these three Greek letters, and that certainly could be a point of distinction. Then I reviewed my list of magazines and saw that there was a problem. I had listed one magazine about the world, one about "Americans," and two about black folks. It was the sixties, and I knew there was some discomfort about racial politics in the nation. So I added *Life* magazine, as an integrationist impulse in case he had been offended by *Ebony* and thought I didn't like white people. This tilted the heretofore balanced list toward him. Three about white folks, two about blacks. What an impressive indication this could be of my racial sensitivity and openness. I thought I had created the perfect list— appropriately political and culturally informed—a list that acknowledged his authority and still one that would be a credit to the race. The moment fades, but the exercise is preserved in the card he returned to us at the end of that school year.

It is clear today that despite my interpretation of the assignment, his directions were to list the magazines we "read" that came to our homes. Not our subscriptions. Not the ones that lay fanned out as decoration on the coffee table. Not the ones that recalled fraternity days only my father would have some interest in remembering. The difference between his assignment and the list I submitted leads me to this forty-something-years-late confessional: I know for sure that I looked at the pictures in *Ebony* and *National Geographic,* that I paused long enough to wonder why there was a relationship between the two words in the title of *Scientific American* but I never got past its cover page, and that even though I read the first-person narratives and humor in *Reader's Digest,* I did not include the magazine on the list because my criteria had little to do with what I actually read. I labored over that fiction of a list and turned it in with not a twinge of anything other than the hope he would believe me. The effort actually may have been the most dedicated and thoughtful one I put forward in that class during the whole school year. Other than Abercrombie and Minerva, it is my only memory from seventh-grade English.

My guilt is not, however, an overwhelming burden. I've far too many other candidates for that distinction. And today I suspect that he knew good and well that I read very little, if anything at all, of what I listed on the file card. And if he was even a little bit strategic, as he most likely was, he may have composed the assignment knowing that he'd discover something other than what he asked for. But I also imagine he had little idea of how his assignment became an exercise where his race and mine mattered.

Had either my science or social studies teacher given me this assignment, it would have been a different exercise altogether. Both were black women, impressive, serious, certainly not given to drawing cartoon characters, and absolutely not candidates for the fiction of a list I went home and created. And it wasn't only that both of them knew my parents and therefore were privy to what magazines might come to our home; it was that I felt, as black women, they already knew me better than my cool white English teacher did.

At first glance there may seem little reason for a fifty-something English professor to remember and recount what seems a vignette from her past, but these days, after a lifetime of reading, teaching from, pondering, writing about, and writing books, I have discovered that encapsulated in that vignette there is a "rest of the text." It tells a story about black folk and reading that hasn't yet made it to our library shelves.

At this twenty-first-century moment in social and cultural history, it may seem as if the story of African Americans in the United States has been fully told—in the narratives of the enslaved and the analyses that have followed these, in the histories and social science studies of the emancipated, through the arts and by its critics, and in the novels and essays, poems and dramas of creative writers. Despite the over-sized and beautifully crafted pictorial histories, the learned tomes that repeat and review the eras of Jim Crow and civil rights and black power, the art books that collect and comment on our images, the music books that recall our songs and their traditions, the illustrated children's books, and indeed all the books, nonfiction and fiction both, that hold the stories and experiences and imagination by and about black folk, there is still a missing text. And this text can be revealed in what we say, what we write, and what we display about our reading. There is something public in a book. Anyone who has ever carried a book onto a bus or plane, or into a meeting, or placed one on her dashboard or front seat, cover deliberately in view so that passersby might take note of the title, knows that "something public" about a book attaches itself to its reader.

Any such public potential for black Americans carries an implicit cautionary note. In eras in which some have thought about why they might not want to wear red, and others have developed a practiced public elocution that resists the stereotypes in black dialects, and others have memories of being told to "act your age, not your color," and goodly numbers of other black folk have engaged in a wide range of public conduct that implicitly acknowledges that there are still too many whites ready to formulate a judgment based on color rather than character, the potential for a book in a person's hands to pronounce some message about the one who carries it is worthy of attention. *BookMarks* explains how African Americans have noticed this potential, made good use of it, and historically have had good reason to make their marks with a list of the books they have read.

What does it mean to have black bodies and books read as a single narrative? Here we might recall the history of the intersection. Whether it was an enslaved African who lost life or limb because she dared to read, or laws that made literacy illegal, or citizens who staged anti–Jim Crow demonstrations in local libraries to protest the back doors or the inaccessibility of these facilities, the matter of books and reading marks the experience of black folk in America in a way that is deeply political and resonantly personal. If, for example, you were a black child in the South in the 1950s and eager to learn, you felt the impress of this experience each school year. You knew the books that were passed on to you could be yours only after they were no longer good enough for the white children who held them first. You received them only after their pages were ripped and their covers too worn. Even though getting books in those magical first days of the school year was a ritual you loved, you knew as well the habit of those other children to leave their mark in these books—the racial epithets that lay in wait for you. Perhaps you would forget the insult the pages might shelter until one day, when you turned a page, you saw a message that made you shudder and made you angry. You were a child who knew the potential of a book's mark.

Blacks in the United States developed an intimate relationship to books because of the way books came to personify a story of race, whether or not their text told that story. For example, when Frederick Douglass writes in his famed *Narrative* a story about the importance of his reading *The Columbian Orator,* it is not just the happenstance of memory that encourages the long recollection he includes in that autobiography—the one, as he noted in its title, that was "Written by Himself." I have always thought this at least a quaint self-referential phrasing, nearly an afterthought in its placement. But I wonder now if positioning "himself" into the very title of the book was an indirect way of calling attention to the intimacy between the two that Toni Morrison, a century later, crafts into that provocative instruction from her novel *Jazz,* to "look where your hands are now."

Douglass uses this story of his life to call attention to his own habits of reading. When he specifically recalls from one of the books he read,

The Columbian Orator, a "dialogue between a master and his slave," it is a moment that allows him to record the important consequence of an event when "the slave was made to say some very smart as well as impressive things in reply to his master—things which had the desired though unexpected effect; for the conversation resulted in the voluntary emancipation of the slave on the part of the master."[1] Douglass's mention of the *Orator* and its liberatory consequence seems a strategic and hopeful instruction to his white readers about his own intelligence and potential. And he makes this point with a marked reference to a book. *BookMarks* explores the life stories, in memoir, autobiography, and public interviews, by black writers who include sentences, paragraphs, and even pages about the books they have read.

A Common Text

When the unnamed narrative voice of Morrison's novel *Jazz* instructs us to "look at where your hands are now," the reader is directed to her own body—to see how her hands grasp the text. The narrative voice directs us to a certain intimacy that returns our attention to the physical act of reading. It reminds us that we too have hold of this story.

The intimacy of this reminder is a metaphor for the relationship that exists between a body and text—an acknowledgment that text can incorporate desire. It may be a reflection of my own desire that I read Morrison's *Jazz* as a novel about a melancholic longing for some body. But I suspect it is not just my own yearning. When I consider that narrative urge to notice the intimacy it makes apparent between body and book, I see there my own brown hands holding a story about a brown girl who died too soon. The common reader in me pauses to notice and to embrace the relationship this encourages. The touch of one to the other—book to body. The racially mindful reader in me knows that the history and the practice of story in black literature acknowledge a particular relationship between black bodies and text, and I wonder which notice this author encourages—the touch or its history? The traditions of books and reading in African America have had a peculiarly interesting history in which the very presence of one marks the potential of the other.

Even though literacy might be assumed and respected by readers of black letters, African American autobiographers and memoirists in the twentieth century continued a version of marking their literate authority with what seems as full an effort of calling attention to their accomplished mastery of books as was present in Douglass's era and as was evident in my studied approach to my English teacher's assignment. Like my audience of one English teacher, the audiences for these autobiographies were, especially early in the century, predominantly white. Once the assumption of literacy was no longer the sole mark of an "exceptional Negro," black authors found a way to signal their authority to these audiences by including, in their narratives about themselves, detailed and specific lists of the books they had read. These lists are so frequently a feature of black autobiography and memoir that they attach to the cultural distinction of this genre, and their consistency operates, in a sense, as a bookmark.

The habit of the booklists that appear in black letters might be understood as a remnant from that earlier tradition of remarking on one's own literacy, but it also registers as an updated version of a claim to having mastered the best of the intellectual habits of an educated elite. The list testifies to the readers that its writer has a familiarity with those authors who are among the most highly valued in literary cultures. Black writers are certainly not alone in commenting on their literary lineages or in recording the books that have mattered in their adolescence or to their professional lives, but the purpose of such commentary and its pattern—annotated in the form of a list of books and authors read—seems deliberate in its effect and intent. Black writers who mark their literary histories in this way indicate that if there remains some lingering skepticism about the authority of their literacy, it might be best contradicted with a lofty list of great books.

Place Matters

If we wonder at all about the reason for or the presumption of these lists, we have to accompany those questions with a consideration of the spaces of reading in the United States, and the impact of reading despite or within the twentieth century's segregated spaces. The public spaces of libraries represented their own versions and methodologies of Jim Crow politics. How could we not imagine some impact on the reading habits of populations targeted by such policies? Some who yearned for the library's resources had to negotiate their passion between supportive neighborhood institutions and dismissive ones farther into town. Others understood that although they were reading liberally and often in libraries that would both service their needs and inspire their creativity, their access was but a matter of location or clime. In 1930, Louis Shores, the librarian at Fisk University, surveyed cities that had significant African American populations. Among the major cities in which no library service was available to blacks were Charleston, Dallas, Mobile, Miami, Raleigh, and Shreveport. Shores found that other cities such as New Orleans and Atlanta offered separate and unequal facilities to black citizens. They had "Negro" branch libraries whose collections and facilities were paltry in comparison to those of the white branch libraries. Cities such as Boston, Chicago, San Francisco, and Seattle offered unlimited service, but some of them would not hire black librarians—using various explanations such as the one offered in Kansas City, Missouri, whose Negro branch librarian was white "because they have never found an efficient colored one. Have tried three." The librarian who answered Shores's inquiry added that "a Negro could never work at main or in a white branch." The excuse offered in my home town of Buffalo, New York, was that "we have not found that mixed staffs work out well for either the staff or the service."[2]

The importance of access to these spaces and their resources is profound, so when black writers of the twentieth century write about their experiences in libraries and the ways in which these spaces have made a difference and had an impact on their reading, readers must appreciate how fragile a location they have inhabited. The habit of the booklist may have emerged as a consequence of black writers' vulnerable relationship to public libraries and as a way to contradict the value that those segregated spaces explicitly assigned. That so many of these writers recall the libraries in which they accomplished their reading, or that denied them access, is not just the occasion of finding the familiar within the expected. Instead, the memories about the locations and the places of the books that made their way onto the reading lists indicate how deeply the authors' relationship with books is related to race—whether the libraries themselves became a hurdle to their reading habits, or a help.

When twentieth-century writers such as Maya Angelou and James Weldon Johnson, Audre Lorde, Langston Hughes, Sonia Sanchez, and James Baldwin nod toward the traditions of the century before, when the judgments about literacy and black folk were linked by law and custom, they document the persistence of some relationship between personal value and an erudite and elite literacy. In a particular kind of writing—autobiographies, memoirs, and personal essays—lists of the books these writers read and memories of the places where their reading mattered signal how their lives and legacies not only are held within the pages of the books they wrote but are embedded as well in the books they have read.

ॐ

When I considered the list of magazines my English teacher would review, I was conscious of how they would, especially in the beginning of the semester and before he knew anything at all about me, mark me as a certain kind of student. What image did I want to convey? Every item I chose to include on that list weighed that question. And even at that young age, while thinking about the pictorials in *National Geographic* and the photo spreads of *Ebony,* my consideration was seriously engaged with my race—and his. It was my chance for creativity as much as it was my opportunity for control.

I suspect that today if you were to ask me what I was reading, I'd form my answer either carefully or casually. The "you" that asks would be determinative. Someone from my book club—a group of women who know me well and whose judgment I could not shape even if I wanted to? The executive of a search firm? A graduate student? A colleague? Someone from my church? A member of the media? Which media—the *New York Times* or the *Amsterdam News?* My daughter? I read a lot of books at a time. And given the audience, I'm likely to select any one of them for the answer to the inquiry.

Of course and certainly there is nothing *necessarily* racialized about the question. And I imagine that whoever asks might not, like my seventh-grade teacher, even think I would place the inquiry into a racialized space. But for African Americans whose lives are unquestionably spent within and without the veil of race, this double consciousness, this "looking at oneself through the eyes of others," as W.E.B. Du Bois explained in *Souls of Black Folk,* is still a powerful vector. And if my answer has either the opportunity, or the potential consequence, of marking me in a certain way, you can be assured that I want that control just as much as I did in seventh grade.

What book am I reading now? It depends.

1

Reading and Desire
in a Room of Their Own

I would not know the thing I sought until I found it. It was both something within and something without myself. Within it, it was like a buried memory that will not come to the tongue for utterance.

J. SAUNDERS REDDING, *No Day of Triumph*

I SAT down at one of the desks in the children's room of our small suburban library in North Carolina. It was in the months soon after our move there—the library having already become a familiar destination. My daughter Ayana had been there all afternoon, and I had gone to pick her up. As I sat cautiously in one of the too-small-for-me chairs at the children's table, she waved at me from a distance, then disappeared behind a shelf of books. I wasn't alone very long. A freckle-faced little girl with wispy auburn hair came and sat next to me. She turned to me with all the deliberate engagement of an eight-year-old (or thereabouts) and said, I know you are that girl's mom, pointing to where Ayana had been just a moment ago. I nodded that I was. So, will you tell me about your village in Africa? I looked around to see who else she might be talking to. Excuse me? I asked. You know. The village where you come from where all the girls and mothers gather to talk and no one else can listen to them because they have their own secret place for meeting? I was going to need help with this, so I looked around for Ayana and was relieved when I saw her rapidly walking toward us. She had already spied the two of us talking, and she was coming in our direction so quickly that the stack of books she carried in her little brown arms was in an extremely precarious balance. You know, the girl insisted, trying to focus my attention back on her, you know how you all sit together and each girl and her mother are next to each other but there are no men and boys because they don't know where you are when you all go away to . . . —Hi! Ayana said breathlessly. Sorry—she turned to her friend with an insistence in her voice beyond her years—my mom and I have to go. I looked at her, puzzled, said goodbye to the girl, and turned to ask my daughter exactly which village in Africa was I supposed to tell her about? And what gathering of mothers and daughters could this be?—me who had never been close to any country in Africa but had surely wanted to go. But then I knew the question I should have asked her.

What book are you reading?

It wasn't her fault; in fact, I like to claim responsibility for her imaginative spirit. I certainly could not claim her pragmatism. She had developed that same habit that my mother had discovered early in me — but she had taken it a bit further than I ever did. My mother always knew what I was reading by the tone of my voice or order of my words. When my father was not home right away from work, she would remind me that he would be home soon and no he had not gone off to war and you only have two sisters, and neither of them is named Meg or Jo. Or if I were to say to her, Please mum, might I have some more? Her reply would be something like, Oh, so it's Dickens today? She'd recognize my source in a minute, knowing that whatever had engaged me did not just spring out of my head, fully formed. It had come instead from some book I was reading that had attached itself to me, spilling out in whatever casual conversation I was having with my mother at the moment. I don't recall doing this with my sisters or father, only my mother, probably because at any moment, as surely as she might acknowledge my source or reground my residence in the present day, she could just as easily respond back to me, her own language fully embellished with whatever century or clime I might have adopted.

So it was not a total surprise to see this bookish creativity develop in my daughter. Ayana was generally the pragmatic type, everywhere except in the library, where she'd disappear into her reading and, as on this occasion, pull any or all of us into whatever was the imaginary of the moment. So when I came to pick her up, I'd certainly recognize what she looked like, but the mind of the child I birthed and was raising could have been left on any shelf in the children's room and coming toward me would be an embodiment from the last book she had read before we were to go home.

In those spaces, between children's chairs and shelves, and bulletin boards meant to alert us to whatever seasonal theme filled its spaces, I jealously watched her transform as she slipped between rows of books as easily as she slipped from one character to the next — whatever she was reading, she took it in and lived it in her head. I only caught glimpses of her transformations, the way she'd grasp a book in her arms and hunch over it as if she and it together made their own room. Once in a while though, something was bound to slip out. As it had to the girl with the wispy red hair looking increasingly puzzled as Ayana pulled me away from what had been her own personal story time with a stranger.

Ayana labored over her occupation with books; she was intense and delighted with the solitude they offered her. It was her ideal space, and we spent much time, whether during school days or summer, collecting armloads of books to bring home so that she might re-create the allure of the library's shelves in the closet of her own room. There was no attic in our house for her to disappear into. So her oversized closet was the recess she had chosen, and there were more books than clothing lining the walls, and a plump yellow beanbag chair that would welcome and embrace and take in whatever shape or fantasy was hers for the moment.

Displacement and Desire

Had she known then of Jessie Fauset's house, my daughter would have understood the metaphor. As the child of a Philadelphia minister, the adolescent Fauset mirrored the classed hierarchy of the "Philadelphia Negro," and her graduation from the elite Philadelphia School for Girls and subsequent Ivy League education—Cornell, and then the University of Pennsylvania—make apparent that she could claim familiarity with the bookish traditions inherent in an elite schooling. Fauset's booklists, therefore, that find their way into the rooms she composed in her 1914 essay "My House and a Glimpse of My Life Therein," seem not an entire fiction.

The essay was first published in the *Crisis*—the organ of the NAACP that would, within five years, appoint Fauset its literary editor. "My House" is one of the earliest publications of this prolific author. In it, she introduces her readers to a fictive house from a distance —"far away on the top of a gently sloping hill"; then, like the close-up in a film, Fauset brings the reader right up to its walls, nestled "in stately solitude" on an idyllic hillside between a valley and forest. It is, she writes, "barely visible through the thick ivy," a prelude to a mysterious setting that quickly becomes suspect. She describes it as "an irregular, rambling building . . . built on no particular plan . . . following no order save that of desire and fancy."[1]

I paused over Fauset's use of the word "desire," thinking again of my own relationship to books and words, sensing its particular appropriateness there in the clutch of language and sense that belongs to a reverie about reading. Desire notices and makes way for a reader's need of intimacy. It resists regulation and order, preferring instead the secure disarray of creativity and imagination. So when Jessie Fauset writes a lush reverie about a house that relinquishes its controlled architecture to her fanciful inhabitations of its rooms, she lays claim to the confusion that desire crafts: "peculiarly jutting rooms appear, and unsuspected towers and bay windows,—the house seems almost to have built itself and to have followed its own will in so doing." Her essay is soon overtaken by a language that overwhelms in its luxury and licentiousness and "the place becomes transformed." With an unapologetic authoritative license, Fauset claims the fictive spaces she has constructed as her own. "My House" then takes a turn that places it fully within the tradition of *BookMarks*—as she names not only the location but the titles of books and their authors, which she knows at least well enough to include in this place of desire, and, we suspect, even more intimately than this. For Fauset, the place she imagines is deeply textured and filled with books. She writes: "Up to the top of the house I go, to a dark little store room under the eaves, I open the trap-door in the middle of the ceiling, haul down a small ladder, mount its deliciously wobbly length, and behold, I am in my chosen domain. . . . I descend to my library, there to supplement my flitting ideas with the fixed conception of others."

As the essay begins, Fauset seems to know and acknowledge the place assigned to her gender, race, and generation. But I think it more likely that she purposefully embraces a cautious and even deferential respect toward the authors who line these bookshelves. She begins with a list of books that appears quite ordinary, books that credibly shape a generationally and gender-appropriate domestic space for her and her reading. But this opening seems merely a device, because once she has gained the reader's comfort through this unimposing setting, she deftly abandons its domestic design and eases her way into the claim of a literary pedigree that will distinguish her. She slips into this assertiveness. When the essay begins, Fauset's claim is genteel, nearly masked in a domestic and even adolescent surround, with a "broad, old-fashioned fireplace . . . on the rug in front I lie and read, and read again, all the dear simple tales of earlier days, *Mother Goose, Alice in Wonderland, The Arabian Nights.*" She continues her list of books in a way that at first demurs from knowing too much—even though it becomes obvious that she knows these texts well enough to order them in particular ways, and to subtly use their order and company to mark her own intellectual curiosity and her familiarity with them as she labors over the detail in these rooms. The embellished detail allows her to assert her familiarity with the rooms and, implicitly, with the books they hold. Readers might suspect here that the metaphor of the attic is a device that masks another claim. By the essay's end, Jessie Fauset is not subtle at all in making evident her occupation of an earned space:

> This is my *living*-room, where I spend my moods of bitterness and misunderstanding, and questioning, and joy, too, I think. Often in the midst of a heap of books, the Rubaiyat and a Bible, Walter Pater's essays, and *Robert Elsmere* and *Aurora Leigh* . . . I jot down all the little, beautiful, word-wonders, whose meanings are so often unknown to me, but whose very mystery I love. I write, "In Vishnu Land what Avatar?" . . . and all the other sweet, incomprehensible fragments that haunt my memory so.

These are likely not as incomprehensible as Fauset's putatively humble representation implies. She confounds what we might expect next and teases her readers just as we begin to suspect that the distinctions she is making between one set of readings and the other indicate an expertise that she has masked.

I imagine her cautiously considering the impact of this essay's publication in the legendary *Crisis,* knowing that she was fully aware how it might help her gain a certain stature within the carefully protected communities of the black intellectual elite. But I suspect as well that she was fully aware of the gendered imbalance of this community and how she would have to manage her debut without offense to its established male intellectuals. So her initial reverie over books, which one might easily dismiss as flirtatious and unsophisticated, seems instead clever and skillful. Fauset seems well aware of what place she might occupy as these books testify to her literary pedigree. The story of the minister Elsmere who loses his faith, in Mary Ward's *Robert Elsmere* (a book that created a sensation in readers in England and the United States after its publication in 1888), finds itself in the same company with the Bible and Elizabeth Browning's epic poem *Aurora Leigh,* about a woman who educates herself with books found in crates in her father's attic. It is not too difficult to imagine that Fauset is using *Aurora Leigh* to suggest—to readers in the know—a link between its content and her own experience. So when she writes a bit further on in "My House" of the books that are too "high" for her to know, it is reasonable to bring a certain skepticism to these passages: "high up on many of the shelves in many rooms are books as yet unread by me, Schopenhauer and Gorky, Petrarch and Sappho, Goethe and Kant and Schelling; much of Ibsen, Plato and Ennius, and Firdausi and Lafcadio Hearn,—a few of these in the original. With such reading in store for me, is not my future rich?" Fauset knows more than she pretends here. "Much of Ibsen" seems a carefully turned phrase that is less likely to describe what's on someone's bookshelves than an answer to an implicit question about what books someone has read. "A few in the original" similarly appears to answer a question not asked and suggests a command of the language of the classics—Latin and Greek—both of which were required courses in Fauset's area of concentration as an undergraduate. Hearn, who was briefly married to a black woman and who wrote newspaper columns replete with dark revelations about poverty in Cincinnati and slave rebellions and ghosts in New Orleans, seems to stand in for the notions of both displacement and desire—he was an author in search of location and self, perhaps more like Fauset than even she anticipated at the time. But she knew enough of his work and seemed to feel enough of an affinity to include him on her list. The list here seems a cipher for a literary history that needed a fiction in order for her to claim it.

Even without a phrase like Douglass's reflexive "written by himself," Fauset embraces the relationship between story and self that Douglass claimed. She concludes her essay with a focus on and an insistent declaration of ownership in which she makes a series of claims, each of which repeats the possessive of the title—and in their repetition she indicates the emphasis of ownership: "can such a house as this one of mine . . . it is so eminently and fixedly mine, my very own, . . .—a house not yours or another's but mine . . . [and] this, then, is my house, and this, in measure, is my life in my house."

Although these phrases are overwritten and mannered to a fault, the reader would err in losing Jessie Fauset's persistent claim of ownership, which connects this fiction to her membership in a literary lineage that is informed, strategic, and intimate.

Fauset's library is a construct of her desire to have her readers see her as gifted and substantially educated and to consider her reasonably placed within the history of books and letters that makes American intellectuals and citizens. There is no explicit mark of race within this construction—its publication in the pages of the *Crisis* accomplishes the racial mark for her. Given her elite education, there is little reason to doubt the authenticity of her list. The fairy-tale-like environs that begin the essay and that seem characteristic of the stereotypes of women's stereotyped interest in the fanciful rather than the real disappear by its end, as if she is unable or, as I prefer to imagine, unwilling to sustain the mask of the fiction and the conventions it embraces. The lists of books at the essay's end displace the earlier pastoral imagery, the "green, green sward . . . under blossoming trees . . . the blending of wind-song . . . the gorgeous rosebushes and purple lilacs . . . the lofty trees . . . tall spires and godly church steeples . . . an enchanted forest." The house reveals itself as not just the imaginary of mind but its decided accomplishment. Her essay concludes with her declaration of its "vivid, permeating, and yet wholly intellectual enjoyment of [its] material loveliness and attractiveness." Fauset's language here is deeply sensual, and its resonance with her desire that her work be perceived worthy of inclusion is unambiguous.

"My House" is written by a youthful Fauset, but its claims make us aware that she imagines a future "rich" in intellectual endowment. Although this is a boastful statement, if readers have understood and appreciated Fauset's literary heritage, they cannot dismiss the assertion that concludes her booklists. She would become, in the years following this publication, well known as an essayist and novelist, and also for her editorship at the *Crisis*. But this essay was a debut piece — and it seems she deliberately selected the opportunity to artfully introduce herself to the magazine's readers as a person familiar enough with literature's entitlements to place herself within that tradition. Given the amount of nonfiction published in the *Crisis,* she could easily have written a piece like one W.E.B. Du Bois penned several years later in which he tutored the magazine's readers on the proper contents of a good library. But she chose instead a fictive moment, and the opportunity this genre afforded her, to make herself both its subject and its object — and so with this gesture she embraced exactly the intimacy that the desire conditions.

A Residence in Books

Many years later, Marita Golden writes of her own attic space. She clothes it in no fiction but recalls this childhood memory in her autobiography, *Migrations of the Heart.* Unlike the rambling disorder of Fauset's fictive house, Golden's childhood home is a "proper" Victorian house "that demanded a certain majesty of their owners."[2] And even though her memories of the house were not at all fanciful (she writes of the "frenzy of cleaning" demanded on Saturday mornings), she finds, as did Fauset, an attic that allowed her a residence dedicated to books. Golden writes:

> In the summer I took up residence in the attic. In its cool, spacious recesses I pasted pictures from *Life* and *Look* on the walls. Under a loose

floorboard I hid reams of poetry and my diary, which charted my anguished journey into adolescence. Most of all, I read books for comfort and salvation.

Her representation of this interior hiding space is different in tone and intent from Fauset's. Years removed from the era of women's suffrage and the yoke of gentility and caution that marked Jessie Fauset's claim to a mind of her own, Golden writes of her own childhood desire to retreat from the perplexities and strains of her family's tensions, and the solace she found not only within the protected and isolated space of the attic but within the similar sanctuaries of books.

> Leaning against the walls in that secret womb, I read *Ivanhoe, Vanity Fair, Tom Jones, Oliver Twist.* For two weeks my heart bled over the fate of Emma Bovary. One summer I lay stretched out on blankets there and read all of Jane Austen and Charlotte Brontë. Books simply saved me. Between their pages I transcended the horrors of my parents' marriage and the stark loneliness that regularly ambushed me.

Her adolescent reading list remembered here contains thick tales of historical romance and fiction. There are novels that demand a sustained attention and, with that focus, allow an explicit escape—mirroring the attic space of her retreat.

Golden's autobiography is notable as well for the strategic way in which she uses books to mark the stages of her life. A list that appears later in its pages effectively traces the civil rights politics of the 1960s as they began with the emergence of a political consciousness, through its attention to social revolution, and then a progression into black arts. She writes that "in high school, we read Sartre. In college we tossed him aside and reached for Mao and Che Guevara. Summer afternoons were spent . . . reading Don Lee and Gwendolyn Brooks." By the close of *Migrations,* a mature Golden reflects on "her present state of mind," using two books, Judith Rossner's *Attachments* and Flaubert's *Madame Bovary,* to represent her development. As different as these books are from each other, they both are concerned with women who take back control of their lives from a society that would restrict and direct them. I think of the disordered architecture from which Fauset wrests her own control, and find Marita Golden and Jessie Fauset not as far removed from each other as the years between them might suggest.

> I have just finished reading Judith Rossner's *Attachments* and rereading *Madame Bovary,* two books that pretty accurately reflect my present frame of mind. Reading Rossner's powerful weaving of mutual dependencies and her dissection of human frailty was like drinking one of those mixed drinks that look harmless. . . . I read *Madame Bovary* for the first time when I was sixteen and appreciated it as just a wonderful love story. Now, at twenty-nine, I know better. . . . My own life of late has begun to resemble the lives of Rossner's two heroines and Emma Bovary as well. . . . It feels like one of those episodic novels by Fielding or Thackeray . . . but since this is my life and not a novel, I can't scratch out whole sections that seem absurd.

Golden's 1987 autobiography indicates its departure from and its legacy in the investment of using books to mark a cultural as well as a personal politic. She makes it evident that she has the credentials of the 1960s black arts/civil rights generation when she notes that she read black arts poets Lee (known in later years as Haki Madhubuti) and Brooks. The authors she marks for inclusion in the autobiography implicitly announce these politics of the era and stand in place of an extended explanation of these politically charged years. Later, in her adult references to Rossner and Flaubert, she claims a space unmarked for race but one that is gendered in a way that reflects both a 1980s attention to feminism and perhaps a personal liberation from the troubled relationship between race and gender politics.

The books she turns to as an adult are disorderly novels whose heroines repudiate social regulation. The reader understands the way in which Golden, in her naming of the novels, uses the moment to mark a self-indulgence that privileges the personal, even in the space of a public autobiography. As if to underscore this indulgence, Golden's mention of the final two books in her autobiography is pulled away from the public address of that genre and placed into the intimate, and otherwise private space of an epistle—a letter that she writes to her mentor and reproduces in this book in italics. Even the form of the letter works to indicate the interior she probes here, and exposes by claiming her nearness to (and distance from) these books.

Despite the scores of years that separate them as well as the differences of era, experience, and generation, Marita Golden and Jessie Fauset share the habit of a booklist. In attic rooms, the creative and appreciable consequences of desire found expression in the quiet, unregulated passions of reading. Their readers certainly learn something important in knowing how each writer cherished her habits of reading, but Fauset and Golden's booklists accomplish more than this. The books that emerge, including works by authors such as Flaubert and Dante, Ibsen and Dickens, indicate precisely what readers of African American autobiography and memoir might not have suspected —and this information is both the impact of the bookmark and its intent.

ع

The lock between desire and intimacy is a critical dimension of the relationship that binds a writer and a reader. It is an enactment of the recollection, at this book's opening, of Toni Morrison's final lines in *Jazz*—lines that position her reader's hands and the narrator's voice together, and asks the reader to notice that closeness. Reading encourages an intimacy like Ayana's hunch over the book in her lap or her collapse into a small brown ball of body and book, where the distinction between the two of them dissolves.

I don't know what desire might have prompted Ayana that afternoon in the library, nor do I recall what she was reading. I remember the moment more for my own failure to engage her fantasy with that little girl, to sit there and explain to her about the village ritual gathering of mothers and daughters—it was at sunset, I would have added. Then I would have reminded Ayana, and her new friend, that we would do each others' hair at that gathering, and how we would create new patterns of braids and agree upon a name for our design, and that we only read fiction when we gathered at those late-in-the-day moments, where we talked together about what our reading and our day has been like. It would have sounded a lot like my current book club, where the notion of women's gathering, bringing tales of our sharing and growing together for review, commentary, or support may have been a model for Ayana, who was sent off to her room when we met at our home. And in my years' later overanalysis of the moment, I wonder if it even reflected her desire to be within rather than outside of this gathering. What she imagined for the little girl seems exactly like the space we "Friday night women" have claimed and agreed to share together, monthly. I know now that I would have, should have transported it to wherever in Africa that Ayana would have desired. Our freckle-faced audience of one would have been fascinated at our story and envious of the closeness that only my daughter and I could share—and then we would have gone home and likely not spoken a word about it. We would have left our fiction to its own end.

I lost my chance at that moment to do for her as my own mother would—talking back to me in an affected British accent, giving me a knowing smile, or even better, from my perspective, just leaving me alone with my fantasy—neither disrupting its hold nor challenging its right to occupy my mind at that moment. Ayana took one look at the quizzical expression I had as I looked at the little girl as if she had lost her mind—what village?—and looked at my daughter to see what haunt had overtaken my child's body. She knew what was coming and understood immediately that we had to go. How I regret today that lost opportunity to have left her desire to its own creation.

2

A Negro Library

When and where I enter . . . the whole Negro race enters with me.

ANNA JULIA COOPER, *A Voice from the South*

SOME judgment about character, conduct, or potential follows closely with the public announcement of what we read. The 1992 photograph of then candidate Bill Clinton with a copy of Walter Mosley's novel and Clinton's follow-up comment that Mosley was among his favorite authors anticipated the comparisons to come of Clinton as America's first "black president." As I recall the photograph, the ever politic Clinton, in full campaign mode, was walking toward an airplane with a copy of a Mosley novel cover out so that anyone with even a slight bit of curiosity could easily see what he was reading. I was going to vote for him anyway—but the move was clearly a black-vote attention getter and an opportunity for the media to consider why this book was Clinton's selection and whether or not they would describe Mosley as an "African American" author in their report of the campaign moment. Had the book been by Anne Rice or John Grisham, the author's ethnicity would certainly not have been the mark of the moment.

The associations we make—between our potentials, our bodies, and our characters—with what we read are particularly sharp for African Americans, and I suspect I am not the only black parent who both notices that potential for association and prepares for what we suspect is its eventuality.

When I attended a lecture at Duke University by Henry Louis Gates back in the early 1990s—several years before I accepted a position at the university—I was unable to arrange for anyone to stay home with the children, so I took them with me. Fairly certain that they would not be interested in his lecture, and hoping I could get them to sit through it quietly and draw as little attention to themselves as possible in what would likely be a room full of professors and graduate students, I suggested that they bring along a book. Actually, it probably went more like this: get a book, get in the car. My daughter would have done that anyway; she rarely went anywhere without a book; she was one of those children to whom a book seems an appendage that changes color and shape like hair ribbons or barrettes but that is always present. My son, however, needed a bit more encouragement to think of a book as an alternative to a set of matchbox cars, but he was cooperative and obedient, plus he liked going anywhere at all, so Bem grabbed one and got into the car. I knew for him it might not have been a thoughtful choice—more like which one was nearer to the door. So yes, I did look to see what he had selected. And yes, I was right to think that I would not be the only one interested.

I think I recall correctly that Gates, my two children, and I were among the few, if not the only black faces in the lecture hall. It was early in the days of Duke University's interest in faculty diversity, and it may even have been the occasion of Gates's "job talk" for the position he would eventually take, albeit briefly, as a professor in the English department.

Bem and Ayana quietly found seats at the back. It was a fairly large room with cushy seats, the desktops that pulled up over the arms of the chairs could be played with until the fascination with their moveability wore off, and big windows that could allay any boredom that might threaten. I was relieved. There would be distractions, and of course, they had their books.

The talk was uneventful as far as the children were concerned, but it was probably anything but that for Duke University, which entered a long period of heightened publicity over all matters related to race and faculty hiring that would last long after Gates departed and in some ways would even lead to my own appointment there. I became a visiting professor a couple of years later to cover the classes Gates left behind in the wake of his departure to Harvard. But before any of that drama, and after his presentation to the department and interested others had concluded, we were making our way out of the door, and both children were enjoying the sloping walkway down toward the exit. Bem, enjoying the acceleration of the ramp just a bit more than his sister, nearly ran into one of the professors who was exiting the hall. I remember watching them interact, and now that I'm a professor in that same department, it doesn't surprise me that I recall the encounter as gentle. That's an odd word, I know, but I'm a pretty good judge of folk at initial meetings, and I still think of the demeanor of this man in the same way today—knowing him somewhat better. I remember his bending over to say hello and, in his characteristically quiet voice, asking what book he had in his arms. Bem had chosen a book of myths and legends (or a book of myths and legends had been nearest to the door). It was an oversized, beautifully illustrated book that still sits on the children's bookshelf in the room I somewhat pretentiously, it sometimes feels to me, call the "library" at home—waiting, interminably it seems, for some grandchild some day to reach up there to select a book for me to read to her. It was certainly a book big and unwieldy enough, especially in a little boy's arms, to command attention. So it probably had nothing whatsoever to do with what I imagine it concerned when that professor bent over to see what book Bem carried. I remember hearing him say "Ah, very good"—with an approving tone that meant more to me at the time than it probably should have. We left the lecture hall together, me satisfied that I had contributed to the race and Bem eager to get to the matchbox cars he had stuffed into the car's back seat pocket. I probably should be remembering this moment today for the content of the lecture, if at all, but it lingers in my storehouse of memories about Bem because we were the only black people in the room and we had, in my imaginary, and at least that one time, fulfilled together our responsibility to be a credit to the race.

Today I think I should have let him bring his cars. I am pretty certain that he did not open the book during the entire talk—the play of the seat's sliding desk top and the view from the windows were more likely entertainments. It would have made him happier, even though the encounter at the end of the lecture would have been a different kind of story and not one for this writing. But my apprehension over whatever judgment might be attached to my children unfortunately took precedence over whatever might make them happier on occasions like their forced attendance at a lecture I had to take them to because I could not leave them home alone and I wanted to go. What prevailed instead was my sense of what we might represent to others and how that representation might carry over to the next black person. Now, years later, and with priorities of family and kinship and love that leap over my concerns about stereotypes, that racial sensitivity seems a waste of energy and effort no matter the ways in which it so easily attached to folk in my parents' generation, and indeed in my own. It's why I overtip—concerned that a waiter or waitress will not form a judgment based on my behavior that black women undertip. Interestingly, I don't think I ever entertained the thought that they might form a presumption that we overtip.

Being prepared for the negative, and working to disrupt it before it even occurs, and being armed with a foregrounded awareness of stereotype is not unrelated to the habit of these booklists and the roles they take on as representational rather than just anecdotal inclusions in autobiography or memoir. But I think this preparedness is not only about the negatives they might encounter—disarming the stereotypes of black boys as threatening rather than bookish or black girls as careless rather than circumspect. It seems as much about shouldering, however unnecessarily or tragically, the burden of living a life under a certain kind of racial scrutiny—where, not being quite certain enough someone will wait to form a judgment about your character or potential, you disarm them with a well-placed book. Maybe that's why my library at home is so full of books, generations of books, from parents and grandparents both. They rest in place on their shelves ready for any extremes, a grandchild's curious reach to the children's books, or an adult's purposeful positioning of one of them in some imagined or real racial scenario.

The library in our home is a room with a piano on one wall, a huge window that looks onto the front yard, framed diplomas of my grandparent's college degrees—including degrees of my grandfather's graduation from the "lower" school to the "upper" school at the famous Palmer Memorial Institute—one signed by Charlotte Hawkins and the other by Charlotte Hawkins Brown; and then a wall of bookshelves that nearly reach the top of the ten-foot ceiling. I need a stepstool to get to the top shelves. The books are all cloth (the paperbacks being relegated to a back office, not quite fine enough in my aesthetic for a room I call a library) and are a mix—some from Bem and Ayana's growing-up years, some from my husband's and my graduate and undergraduate schooldays, and books from my parents' and my grandparents' homes. The most treasured volumes in my library are those from my maternal grandparents: a series of "the collected works of . . . " in dark red and faded black binding that sit on the highest shelf, books-in-waiting for a child like I was, bored from a summer away from home and relishing the opportunity to spend my day with the next of an author's works in the collection rather than doing chores my grandmother had waiting. The books from my father's den, mostly art histories, biographies, encyclopedias of music and opera, and histories of war and remembrance fill the shelves beneath this one. They are marked only by my familiarity with their bindings and the places they were shelved in the room my father saved for himself.

I don't know when my language moved from "den" to "library"—one might assume I would call the room a den, as it was designated in my adolescence—but this label was a considered decision. I wanted to create a special room in our home for these books that marked my growing up, my husband's, and that of my children. I thought "den" was neither formal nor expansive enough for the histories of family and event, children's laps and Christmas gifts, that lay within these books, and that "library" would more appropriately designate the distinctive feel that that room has in our home and the responsibility for memories that it contains. Every once in a while I imagine painting some words across the window wall near the ceiling. I imagine them as a gilded script that seems perfectly in place in a room like this one —or in a room like I imagine this one to be. They would be words that suggest something lovely, lofty, and serene, and that capture the feeling I have there when the afternoon sun lingers and stretches across from the antique library desk in the window to the chair where I sit reading. But there are both too many words to choose from, and too few that will hold the heft of children and families and my expectations, all ghosts that inhabit the room.

A Library in (the) *Crisis*

When, in 1931, "a Philadelphia correspondent" to the NAACP wrote
to Walter White, then secretary of the organization, soliciting advice
about what books he might include in his personal "library," the letter writer offered the following description of himself to help shape
whatever might be the journal's response. He wrote that he was "a
Negro Father, twenty-six years of age," and "anxious to include in my
library such books as my limited budget of $1 to $2 a week will allow."[1] W.E.B. Du Bois, as editor of the NAACP's national magazine
the *Crisis,* determined that the letter "deserves to be broadcast" and
responded with a list of books attentive to the reader's request to
"consider meritorious works of any date about the Negro or written
by Negroes." The father had explained his interest to Du Bois, saying,
"In this way I am hoping within the next eight or ten years to possess
a good collection of Negro literature."

It was 1931 in America, still the early years of the economic depression that gripped Americans of all classes and that held African
Americans with special ferocity. These were the years, my mother
told us, when her mother made ketchup soup during too cold Detroit winter days; these days explained for us why a teabag was never
thrown out on first use in our home. The habits of the Depression lin-
gered long past those days.

The pages of the *Crisis* were dedicated to covering this unfolding
tragedy. Du Bois's biographer, David Levering Lewis, wrote that the
magazine would "monitor, expose, and pass judgment" as the "effects
of the Depression worsened month after month, falling upon Negroes
with redoubled intensity."[2] Given the dire straits of most Americans
during this era, and even the financial precariousness of the magazine, this letter from "a Negro Father" is especially interesting—in
terms of both Du Bois's decision to publish it and to respond, as well
as the decision of the letter writer to express an interest in building a
library in the midst of such financially challenging times. It may have
been that the magazine saw this as an occasion to make public and

to reaffirm the intellectual aspirations of the Negro during a period in which most would suspect that the grim economic challenges of the era overrode anything but energies directed toward making ends meet. But Du Bois's tutorial-like response reflected his own deep interests in the development of intellectual aspirations for African Americans and the wider world's notice of these. Perhaps this is why his advice did not expose in any way a concern about the financial challenge of the era. In the response published with the letter in the magazine's March issue, Du Bois told *Crisis* readers that this "is a man of small income, who has got the vision to see that a sum between $12 and $25 a year will be well spent for books." As attentive and thorough as he is in his response, Du Bois cannot, however, manage to restrict his advice to the parameters of the father's request for books about "the Negro or written by Negroes"; nor does he seem to fully appreciate the financial parameters of the project but quickly takes the upper ranges of the budget as his target. Although he suggests a long list of nearly sixty books (including three of his own) that might be acquired over a period of about a decade, Du Bois begins his response to the letter writer with an admonition not to "neglect the daily paper, the weekly paper, and the monthly magazine. He must subscribe to one of the large colored weeklies and at least one colored magazine. Beside that, a weekly, like the *Nation* or *Literary Digest* and a monthly like the *American Mercury, Harper's* or *The Forum* will give the necessary broad outlook of an American citizen."

As sensitive as Du Bois may have been to the situation of the Negro, he doesn't appear to have been particularly thoughtful here about the bounds of the father's request. If the advice about dailies and weeklies and monthlies and a colored magazine had been followed, the letter writer's budget for books would have been seriously constrained. He'd have had just a little over half the amount left that he considered the most he could spend, and four-fifths of the amount of the lower range he considered.

At the time, a "colored" magazine like the *Crisis* cost 15 cents per copy; the *Nation* was another 15 cents, and the *American Mercury*

50 cents. The daily paper would have occasioned another expenditure. The irony of the magazine's own financial constraints, which challenged Du Bois's editorship and management, seems to match his somewhat casual response to the constrained resources expressed within the letter writer's request.

Du Bois is mounting his role as educator here. So it is particularly noteworthy where he chooses to be specific and leave no room for misunderstanding and where his response is more general. He seems to assume that the colored weeklies and magazines need not be named for his magazine's readership, but he specifically names other, non–African American magazines, in the process educating his audience about where in the non–black publishing world money might be spent and education be obtained. He tells this father not to "neglect general literature," naming the "Haldeman-Julius little Blue Books at five cents each, the Modern Library at 75 cents, and other volumes at $1 to $3" that "must be bought now and then."

Emanuel Haldeman-Julius's publishing enterprise in Girard, Kansas, directed its efforts toward educating America's populace in a world literature. Between 1919 and 1951 the plant produced over 500 million blue books, a mass culture sweep that included reprints of works such as Omar Khayyám's *The Rubaiyat,* and authors as diverse as Oscar Wilde, Guy De Maupassant, Edgar Allan Poe, Henry Thoreau, Émile Zola, Thomas Paine, Plato, Boccaccio, Socrates, Leo Tolstoy, Arthur Conan Doyle, and even Margaret Sanger. When early twentieth-century African American writers mention their youthful reading of some of these writers, as they very frequently do, the Haldeman-Julius blue books were their likely source. The accessibility of these books tempers what might otherwise seem an original and self-directed intellectual curiosity that suggested a reading habit that was more selective than might otherwise have been the case had not these books been so popular and ubiquitous.

The Modern Library's reprints of "classic" works were also included among Du Bois's recommendations. After noting the desirability of these others, he finally offered a list of books he represents as "indispensable to a good Negro library—a list of over 60 volumes that might be acquired over the years" and, as he helpfully notes in a postscript, available for purchase from the *Crisis*.

Du Bois's list of indispensable books by and about African Americans is notably *not* an index of the works he writes of as formative in his own education. Here he parallels the habit of other black writers of the twentieth century who, when noting their own literary biographies, infrequently mention black literature. The list he offers to readers of the *Crisis* in 1931 makes apparent the wide selection of works in print about black folk. Acknowledging that his advice begins in a way that does not answer the inquiry, Du Bois then turns his attention directly to the letter writer's request:

> But the specific quest is . . . for Negro literature. Some of these books are recently published, some can only be found in second-hand stores; but all are indispensable to a good Negro library. They can be bought gradually from year to year:

> "The American Negro" published by the Annals of the American
>   Academy
> Balch's "Occupied Haiti"
> Brawley's "The Negro in Literature and Art"
> Buell's "Native Problem in Africa"
> Bullock's "In Spite of Handicaps"
> Chesnutt's Novels
> Cullen's Poems
> Du Bois' "Souls of Black Folk," "The Negro," "Darkwater"
> Fauset's "For Freedom"
> Jessie Fauset's Novels
> Finot's "Race Prejudice"
> Henson's "The Negro Explorer at the North Pole"
> Hill's "Toussaint L'Overture"
> Hughes' Poems and "Not Without Laughter"
> Johnson's Poems and "Black Manhattan"
> Nella Larsen's Novels

Leys' "Kenya"

Life of John Brown

Locke and Montgomery's "Negro Plays"

Locke and others, "The New Negro"

Lugard's "Tropical Democracy"

Lynch's "Facts of Reconstruction"

Mckay's Poems

Kelley Miller's "Race Adjustment"

Moton's "What the Negro Thinks"

Ovington's "Portraits in Color"

Olivier's "The Anatomy of African Misery" and "White Capital and
    Colored Labor"

Pickens' "Bursting Bonds"

Reuter's American Race Problem"

Robeson's "The Life of Paul Robeson"

Simmons' "Men of Mark"

Spero and Harris' "The Negro Worker"

Starr's "Liberia"

Stowe's "Uncle Tom's Cabin"

Toomer's "Cane"

Vandercook's "Black Misery"

Washington's "Up From Slavery"

Wesley's "Negro Labor in the United States"

White's Novels and "Rope and Faggot"

Williams' "History of the Negro Race"

Wilson's "The Black Phalanx"

Woodson's "Negro Orators" and "The Negro in Our History"

Woolf's "Empire and Commerce in Africa"

His is not a list of exclusively black authors, but the subjects—in fiction, poetry, and history—for this "Negro library" are explicitly about the race.

I imagine that readers of the *Crisis,* and one of its former editors especially (Jessie Fauset), would be particularly interested in this list and its potential to identify who's in (and who is not in) the exclusive ranks of "Negro intellectuals." And Du Bois seems to tease this potential. In a postscript following the list he asks, "Have we made serious omissions already? If so, write us." Of course, both the reader and Du Bois know the huge difference between being named on the first list and being written in as a footnote in a later issue.

The list's composition makes its biases apparent—the two women on it and Charles Chesnutt are the only novelists whose works are not explicitly named. I imagine that Jessie Fauset, as a former editor at the magazine, and Nella Larsen were particularly chagrined. Du Bois's "failure to incorporate black women in the sphere of intellectual equality" has been the subject of some academic commentary, especially his erasure and failure to document contemporary women's contribution to the politics of the era, specifically activists like Ida B. Wells-Barnett and Anna Julia Cooper.[3] Neither of them is on the list, but they would certainly have been appropriate. Charles Chesnutt's abbreviated mention is slightly more of a puzzle than the oversight of these women; he was, however, an extraordinarily prolific writer, and it may have been that Du Bois, whose own record at the time was not as noteworthy, did not wish to encourage a comparison. Makers of lists are especially authoritative, and selective. Du Bois's own personality and ego seem exposed in his response to this reader.

It seems not too far-fetched to wonder whether Du Bois was not actually composing a list for a "Negro's" library. His classic work, *The Souls of Black Folk,* makes plain the distance he sees between himself and the "folk." The persona he adopts in that book allows him to condescend to the race without being confused with them. Despite these recommendations for a Negro library in the pages of the *Crisis,* Du Bois had already made apparent his own elite literary company.

The chapter "On the Training of Black Men" in *Souls* contains an encomium to the classic literature that shaped Du Bois's own training—and we see none of those authors represented on the Negro library list. He composed that chapter to extol the virtues of "black men emancipated by training and culture" and to contradict any notion that manual training is an appropriate end for Negro education. Just before he notes the authors who have enabled his own elevation to the "higher individualism that the centres of culture protect," he waxes poetic on the lofty heights that such reading might obtain: "the chance to soar in the dim blue air above the smoke is to their finer spirits boon and guerdon for what they lose on earth by being black." An interesting blend of hubris and braggadocio encourages him to place himself fully within the company of these classic writers, and he does not suggest, either implicitly or explicitly, that the other black folk who are the subject and audience of *Souls* might join the rarified company he assumes. Instead, his comment on books and reading clarifies for his reader the authority he claims in *Souls* to educate, admonish, and instruct. He writes to make apparent and ordinary his own unqualified, comfortable, and authoritative membership in a company of European writers spanning classic literature's ages:

> I sit with Shakespeare and he winces not. Across the color line I move arm in arm with Balzac and Dumas, where smiling men and welcoming women glide in gilded halls. From out the caves of evening that swing between the strong-limbed earth and the tracery of the stars, I summon Aristotle and Aurelius and what soul I will, and they come all graciously with no scorn nor condescension. So, wed with Truth, I dwell above the Veil.[4]

The irony of Du Bois's letter is that it never engages the issue of why a private library such as the one the father wanted to create might stand as an alternative to libraries in communities of *Crisis* readers across the country that were closed to black patrons.

Not So Public Libraries

In remembering the open and welcoming libraries of my youth, I have come to appreciate that particular gift of luxury, knowing now that others of my generation and earlier had very different and troubling experiences with librarians and fractured relationships with libraries. What I took for granted as a child was gained only through stealth by some children, and with bitter encounters and memories by others. While Jessie Fauset invented a library of and in her mind, and the "Negro Father" who wrote to the *Crisis* planned one for his personal use, for many African Americans, in the first half of the twentieth century especially, an imagined library may have been an invention of necessity. For most black children and adults, public libraries were, during the nineteenth and twentieth centuries, foreboding spaces. Libraries have made their own culturally inflected historical marks on the story of the book as commodity and its readers as consumers.

There were far too many places where the matter of a book and reading were racially coded for black children and adults in the United States. In the South especially, main library buildings were often marked by racial dismissiveness, disdain, and denial. As "public" as libraries were declared to be in their presentations, the practice of access was racially constructed. The history of segregation in this country was apparent in reading rooms, as access to them was negotiated through the same screen of racial politics as were other "public" places and services in the United States. In the 1950s the Birmingham Public Library "was open only to white people, but in a hidden room in the building, accessible only through a secret black entrance, a Black librarian had her headquarters. Black people could pass lists of books to her, which she would try to secure from the library."[5]

Just one year after the Negro father's letter appeared in the *Crisis*, Fisk librarian Louis Shores wrote an article titled "Library Service and the Negro," which was published in the *Journal of Negro Education*. Shores observed that "there is a tendency in the North to restrict the Negro reader, and in the South an honest and frank effort to provide segregated facilities."[6] He pointed out the inanity of segregated thinking: "one public library . . . will permit Negroes to borrow books for home use but prohibits reading in the building; another public library has almost the opposite regulation, insisting that Negroes read books in the library but do not take them home." And even where it might seem that branch library service offered the neighborhood opportunities that suggest equity, Shores was appropriately suspicious and critical of the main libraries that did provide branch library service, suggesting that "the creation of Negro branches has been merely the first step toward complete segregation."

Shores imagined a day where "there will be no question about the library's place" and no shadow of its segregated history. The journey toward that goal was difficult, and the public spaces of libraries were among the targeted sites in the civil rights movement. In 1966, in Clinton, Louisiana, the Audubon Regional Library operated three branches and two bookmobiles. The branch libraries were restricted to whites only. The two bookmobiles they operated were segregated: a red one served only whites and a blue one served blacks. It was their nod to the requisite of the 1896 *Plessy v. Ferguson* decision by the U.S. Supreme Court—separate but equal. When Quincy Brown entered the library branch, however, his was not a casual request; he had anticipated the occasion and the response. He was as careful in his approach to what would be an eventual court case as were the NAACP lawyers who had orchestrated the litigation of Louise Brown more than a decade earlier. Four other young men accompanied him and waited while Mr. Brown requested Booker T. Washington's 1909 book, *The Story of the Negro*. There is no additional information about this choice of title, but I cannot help but imagine it a calculated decision—knowing the likelihood of the volume not being in the library. Also, perhaps anticipating the publicity of the case, they likely carefully considered what book they would want to represent the occasion, perhaps even signifying, through this title, the weight of years of black history that the library failed to make available. Did they go through a list thinking about which book might tell the story of the event they were to stage? Were suggestions made and discarded? However the final determination was reached, *The Story of the Negro* was not to be shared with them at Audubon. The librarian responded that she would request it for him through the state library and then mail it to his home. Mr. Brown's protest began at that moment. He quietly joined his companions at the library table, waiting for the librarian to do as they anticipated. And she complied when she asked them to leave because the premises were restricted to whites. As much as we know about civil rights protests and bus boycotts and store sit-ins, there are fewer stories about the libraries that were the location of protest. In this event, the court case that emerged from this protest was finally decided by the U.S. Supreme Court. It held that Quincy Brown had the right to engage in a silent vigil in the public library and that to disallow it would be a violation of his first amendment right to free speech.

At least Brown and his companions had a table and chairs. In 1960, the Danville, Virginia, library created a "stand-up pick-up-your-books-and-go" policy for blacks. The library went so far as to remove tables and chairs so that there would be no place for black patrons to sit.[7] The Greenville, South Carolina, library for blacks was "a little hole in the wall" with few books, although the "colored" librarian could re-quest books from the main library. Activist and scholar Angela Davis remembers how, in Birmingham, her "mother or father picked up my books downtown, or else the Black librarian, Miss Bell, would bring them by the house"—perhaps methods employed by Davis's parents to circumvent her encounters with the racism of the back door. The images across the South and North were similar. Libraries were re-stricted, separate, and meager—or, as in the case of Greenville, shut down. The city's response to the court's determination was to close all of its libraries rather than to permit blacks access to the main li-brary. Although the impeccably dressed and carefully groomed pro-testors for these events made the news, with their images laboring to indicate the respectability of the race that sought access, the legends and records of black protest do not often recall the library spaces they lay claim to with all the process and maneuvers of the era.

The Audubon case, *Brown v. Louisiana,* was decided twelve years after the famous *Brown v. Board of Education* (1954), and it cited *Brown v. Board* in its decision. Public libraries in the United States were not available to all publics, either before or for many years after the school integration case. These restrictions seem a particular legacy of pre–Civil War days, when laws prohibiting the teaching of reading and writing to blacks were one way of maintaining the privileges and dis-tinctions of class. After the Civil War, libraries were segregated, a state of affairs that was supported legally by the "separate but equal"

In 1960, eight students were arrested for trying to integrate the Greenville County Library. Front row (from left), *Joan Mattison Daniel, Elaine Means, Margaree Seawright Crosby, Dorris Wright, Hattie Smith Wright;* second row, *Jesse Jackson and Benjamin Downs;* back row, *Willie Joe Wright and attorneys Donald Sampson and Willie T. Smith Jr. Photo was taken in front of the old Greenville City Jail on Broad Street. Photo courtesy of the* Greenville News.

doctrine upheld in *Plessy v. Ferguson,* and restrictive Jim Crow statutes ruled in cities and counties across the country. The law "placed the responsibility of providing facilities and service to blacks in the hands of each state" and "the responses varied according to local culture . . . accommodations could be separate branches, rooms, entrances, days of service or more often no service at all." Louis Shores's 1935 survey of 565 public libraries in the United States indicated that only 83 of these offered some kind of service to African Americans.[8]

Invisible Man author Ralph Ellison recalls some of this history in his collection of essays, *Shadow and Act.* He writes that if he were asked about his experiences with libraries while he was growing up in Oklahoma City, the question could lead to a

> longish lecture on the Ironies and Uses of Segregation. When I was a small child there was no library for Negroes in our city; and not until a Negro minister invaded the main library did we get one. For it was discovered there was no law, only custom, which held that we could not use these public facilities. The results were the quick renting of two large rooms in a Negro office building (the recent site of a pool hall), the hiring of a young Negro librarian, the installation of shelves and a hurried stocking of the walls with any and every book possible. It was, in those first days, something of a literary chaos.[9]

For many of these writers, the place of reading—whether attic room or children's room—marks a special place in their narratives. Having room to read mattered. Ellison continues the recollection, falling into the tradition of the booklist, annotating the reading he accomplished once there was, literally, a room for reading:

> How fortunate for a boy who loved to read! I started with the fairy tales and quickly went through the junior fiction; then through the Westerns and the detective novels, and very soon I was reading classics— only I didn't know it. There were also the Haldeman Julius Blue Books, which seem to have floated on the air down from Girard, Kansas; the syndicated columns of O. O. McIntyre, and the copies of *Vanity Fair* and the *Literary Digest* which my mother brought home from work.

When African Americans write about their reading in the decades of the twentieth century before *Brown v. Louisiana,* the reading habits they describe often were encumbered by restrictions that led to no library, or to a library with little to distinguish it from just a room with books and shelves. If there was access to a library, it often took an act of courage, or subterfuge, to do something as simple as check out a book. The frequent mention of libraries in these narratives marks a direct association between books and the experiences of segregation. In contradicting the ethic of segregation, books had a weight of their own.

In Memphis, Tennessee, in the mid-1920s, Richard Wright knew well the story of restricted access: he was allowed to use the library to get books for whites, but he could not himself be a patron. In *Black Boy* he writes in excruciating detail of his experience in the Memphis library, beginning this difficult narrative with a matter-of-fact representation of its Jim Crow policy and noting that "there was a huge library near the riverfront, but I knew that Negroes were not allowed to patronize its shelves any more than they were the parks and playgrounds of the city." [10]

The design of the Memphis library followed a tradition of creating magisterial edifices for these buildings. Constructed to resemble temples of learning, and often touting exteriors of elegantly carved stone, these weighty structures combined with the ritual ceremonies of silence demanded in their interiors to establish themselves as sacred spaces. Despite the nature of the Carnegie philanthropy, whose largesse was extended to small towns and cities for the building of public libraries, these often elaborately decorated buildings, created to overwhelm in elegance and effect, were restricted to only a portion of the public. Wright's recollection does not engage this history of design, but the image of this "huge" space, and his labored effort to gain access, makes his library story even more poignant. He writes: "I had gone into the library several times to get books for the white men on the job. Which of them would now help me to get books?"

He makes a decision to solicit their empathy, based on his hope that prejudice against the Irish and Catholics might create a close enough bond. The concern of the Irishman whom Wright approaches

The Cossitt Library in Memphis, Tennessee. Photo courtesy of the Looking Back at Tennessee Collection, Tennessee State Library and Archives.

suggests that he suspects Wright of trying to integrate the library; he wanted no part of that kind of effort, but he could not help but be supportive of Wright's interest in reading generally.

> One morning I paused before the Catholic fellow's desk.
>
> "I want to ask you a favor," I whispered to him.
>
> "What is it?"
>
> "I want to read. I can't get books from the library. I wonder if you'd let me use your card?"
>
> He looked at me suspiciously. . . .
>
> "You're not trying to get into trouble, are you, boy?" he asked, staring at me.
>
> "Oh, no, sir."

The author who inspires this now famous attempt is H. L. Mencken. Wright had read a diatribe against Mencken in the *Memphis Commercial Appeal*. It is likely he was reading an editorial response to one of Mencken's columns on the Scopes trial in July 1925. The trial challenged the Butler Act, a Tennessee statute that prevented teaching in the public schools that man was related to or descended from lower animals. Wright does not mention here the context of the newspaper's column, but it seems clear that whatever was written was enough to provoke his interest that a newspaper had called down "the scorn of the South" on a white man. The librarian asks him:

> "What book do you want?"
>
> "A book by H. L. Mencken."
>
> "Which one?"
>
> "I don't know. Has he written more than one?"
>
> "He has written several."
>
> "I didn't know that."
>
> "What makes you want to read Mencken?"
>
> "Oh, I just saw his name in the newspaper," I said.
>
> "It's good of you to want to read," he said, "But you ought to read the right things."

In other contexts it would be somewhat of a coincidence that both the Irishman who worked at the optical company as well as the librarian would recognize the author's name. But Mencken had made himself infamous in Tennessee with his parodic accounts of the trial and his antipathy for Tennesseans who agreed with the prosecution. Wright's request doubled the layers of scrutiny and suspicion—it was not only that a black youth wanted to read that but he wanted to read about a man most Tennesseans despised.

A few days later he called me to him.

"I've got a card in my wife's name," he said. "Here's mine."

"Thank you, sir."

"Do you think you can manage it?"

"I'll manage fine," I said.

"If they suspect you, you'll get into trouble," he said.

"I'll write the same kind of notes to the library that you wrote when you sent me for books," I told him. "I'll sign your name."

He laughed.

"Go ahead, let me see what you get," he said. That afternoon I addressed myself to forging a note. Now, what were the names of books written by H. L. Mencken? I did not know any of them. I finally wrote what I thought would be a fool-proof note. *Dear Madam: will you please let this nigger boy*—I used the word "nigger" to make the librarian feel that I could not possibly be the author of the note—*have some books by H. L. Mencken?* I forged the white man's name. I entered the library as I had always done when on errands for whites, but felt I would somehow slip up and betray myself. I doffed my hat, stood a respectable distance from the desk, looking as unbookish as possible, and waited for the white patrons to be taken care of. When the desk was clear of people, I still waited. The white librarian looked at me.

"What do you want, boy?" As though I did not possess the possibility of speech, I stepped forward and simply handed her the forged note, not parting my lips.

"What books by Mencken does he want?' she asked.

"I don't know, ma'am," I said, avoiding her eyes.

"Who gave you this card?"

"Mr. Falk," I said.

"Where is he?"

"He's at work at the M—Optical Company," I said. "I've been in here for him before."

"I remember," the woman said. "But he never wrote notes like this."

Oh God, she's suspicious. Perhaps she would not let me have the books? If she had turned her back at that moment, I would have ducked out the door and never gone back. Then I thought of a bold idea:

"You can call him up, ma'am." I said, my heart pounding.

"You're not using these books, are you?" she asked pointedly.

"Oh no, ma'am, I can't read."

"I don't know why he wants books by Mencken," she said under her breath. I knew now that I had won; she was thinking of other things, and the race question had gone out of her mind.

I suspect that instead, the librarian's mind was focused on the matters of the Scopes trial.

Wright's introduction to Mencken, and his strategy for acquiring books, marks his foray into literature. He lists the authors that Mencken notes in *A Book of Prefaces,* his collection of critical essays. It is a provocative title in terms of Wright's pronouncement of it as the book that marked his own literary curiosity. He writes: "Were these men real? Did they exist or had they existed? And how did one pronounce their names?" Wright's list in *Black Boy* are authors whom Mencken references in *Prefaces:* "Who was Anatole France? Joseph Conrad? Sinclair Lewis, Sherwood Anderson, Dostoevski, George Moore, Gustave Flaubert, Maupassant, Tolstoy, Frank Harris, Mark Twain, Thomas Hardy, Arnold Bennett, Stephen Crane, Zola, Norris, Gorky, Bergson, Ibsen, Balzac, Wells, Gogol, T. S. Eliot, Gide, Baudelaire, Edgar Lee Masters, Stendhal, Turgenev, Huneker, Nietzsche, and scores of others?" He writes that reading awakens his "impulse to dream . . . and I hungered for books, new ways of looking and seeing." Wright does note books he read that mattered after this moment with Mencken, but I think it as interesting that he repeats the authors mentioned in *A Book of Prefaces* in much the way that other writers of the era list books that have been on their own reading lists. Wright attends to this tradition of a booklist in black letters, but marks it with an essential difference that prompts the reader to consider what he might have done with the curiosity piqued by reading Mencken. Neither of the authors he specifically mentions later is on the Mencken list. Wright reports that he read Sinclair Lewis's *Main Street* and that "novels created moods in which I lived for days." And he notes that when he read Dreiser's *Jennie Gerhardt* and *Sister Carrie,* these books "revived in me a vivid sense of my mother's suffering." His reading of these books ("deep stuff," in the assessment of one white man who questioned him about his books) meant "it would have been impossible for me to have told anyone what I derived from these novels, for it was nothing less than a sense of life itself. All my life had shaped me for the realism, the naturalism of the modern novel, and I could not read enough of them."

During 1925–1927, Wright's Memphis years, there were, as Du Bois was to document in the *Crisis,* scores of books to be read by and about Negroes. But Wright had no way of knowing this, and he reports that he suspected he was racially isolated in this interest, bemoaning that he "knew of no Negroes who read the books I liked and I wondered if any Negroes ever thought of them. . . . When I read a Negro newspaper I never caught the faintest echo of my preoccupation [with reading] in its pages."

Instead of reveling in the worlds opened to him by reading, as did his contemporaries Fauset (who wrote in the same era) and Du Bois, Wright, through his eventual turn toward writing, glimpses a morose and fatalistic naturalism harbingered in the response he had to his reading: "I held my life in my mind, in my consciousness each day, feeling at times that I would stumble and drop it, spill it forever. My reading had created a vast sense of distance between me and the world in which I lived and tried to make a living, and that sense of distance was increasing each day."

Wright's association between himself and his books seems anything but a version of desire—it instead seems like residue from the associative pressure that comes from living in the midst of readily available stereotypes that might attach to our bodies and, in anticipation of these, having to invent responses that would preserve our integrity. Even when he wrote that "it was not a matter of believing or disbelieving what I read, but of feeling something new, of being affected by something that made the look of the world different," we get no sense of enjoyment or delight from this response to his introduction to books—just a grim fatalism that would eventually characterize a good deal of the books he would write. Nevertheless, like Douglass's earlier use of books to mark the moment of his liberation, Wright also marks reading as liberatory even though it is submerged in what he alleges as its paradoxically pessimistic force: "it had been only through books—at best, no more than vicarious cultural transfusions—that I had managed to keep myself alive in a negatively vital way. Whenever my environment had failed to support or nourish me, I had clutched at books; consequently, my belief in books had risen more out of a sense of desperation than from any abiding conviction of their ultimate value."

Whether that sense extends from the unhappy and tortured experience of having to write of himself as a "nigger" and to get books by subterfuge and self-deprecation is unclear. It would be a stretch (but not a great one) to imagine such a link. Nevertheless, it is clear that some very public experiences with books and reading may follow us in interesting ways. Wright devoted a number of pages in *Black Boy* to this encounter—repeating dialogues in that section ("he said," "she said," "I said") to near distraction—a mechanistic and static prose that appears nowhere else in that otherwise fluid though despairing book. This departure from his otherwise liquid narrative suggests there was something about that encounter that was different from others—even though many of the stories he tells there are heartbreaking and difficult to read—much less to have experienced. His stark but detailed reporting of gaining access to his public library is, at least, a telling curiosity.

ࢶ

There is no particular reason why I should recall that encounter between the professor and Bem—there are so many more important moments in the too short time I had with him that I have forgotten. I long to be able to remember books with him as I have with his sister—to embrace those memories, to smile over their ironies and our shared spaces. But instead, what I have left are books marked with "To BK, Christmas 1990" or "for our son, with love, mom and dad." But even most of those are gone. I look at *The Book of Answers* that we bought for him in 1990—was it a birthday? or Christmas?—was its title a signal to him or about us? I look at *Jambo Means Hello* and *Stories Julian Tells* almost like archived evidence that there was a childhood, even though I cannot recall those days. I have his copy of *The People Could Fly,* but today it makes me remember how I wished at one point he might escape the life his life was becoming and fly back to Africa like those magical ancestors. I did not know then, at the moment of my desperate imaginary, the horror that escape would one day hold for him, and for us.

Slipped beneath the glass that covers my desk is a bookmark that I got at one of those English teachers' conferences many years ago— a score of years and more. Of all the paraphernalia and memorabilia we are wont to collect at conferences, this is the only one I have saved. I remember that I had already read to both Ayana and Bem the book whose publication it announced and that they might be excited if I were to return with these signed bookmarks from its author. And today, I notice that the subtitle of that book (*Poems for Innocent and Experienced Travellers*) seems to tell another tale, one as true as the memories I need that I can hold without anguish. The author's handwriting on this bookmark is nearly as whimsical and fine as the book itself —*A Visit to William Blake's Inn*. Under the glass, I see her signature and his name together—"Nancy Willard" and "to Bem" and her quick sketch of a smiling sun—its ink fading now but still holding a place on that bookmark, still marking some memory of a book we held together. I do think of her sketch as homonym.

I wonder today at how fragile and indeed how fanciful a thing is memory. How it is shaped, like so many of these moments with books, with desire. Perhaps that is why after Bem died I could not read. I remember the shudder when I realized—this is lost too? Read-

ing? The thing that had been a lifetime of solace and escape and se-
duction into another space too is gone, with him? But there was a way
I also understood and thought those losses were not unreasonably
paired. The desire for his body back, the incoherence of those days,
and the disorderly claims of reading find their own fearful symmetry.

It took me years to hold a book again in the way that would allow its story to displace my own, and it has returned gradually, but
frankly, imperfectly. At that moment in the classroom at Duke and
before he was lost to us, I think now I was already worried, focused
on a way to hope that he might become, perhaps, the kind of boy the
professor who stooped to speak imagined in his "Ah, very good." I
suspect I knew then that as beautiful as that book of myths and legends was, he would not find a bookish imagination, and a book would
be neither his fascination nor his refuge.

I am left without my son, whose terrible death maintains its grip
on my spirit. I do have left the sense that books and our memories of
them and their spaces have a potential for both marking and mourning a far greater intimacy than we might at first imagine could come
from our touch of its pages.

3

On Censorship and Tarzan

This criticism is not altered by our grateful remembrance of those who have heroically taken their pens to champion the black man's cause. But even here we may remark that a painter may be irreproachable in motive and as benevolent as an angel in intention, nevertheless we have a right to compare his copy with the original and point out in what respects it falls short or is overdrawn; and he should thank us for doing so.

ANNA JULIA COOPER, *A Voice from the South*

SOME time in the 1960s my mother wrote a letter to the editors of the textbook company Scott Foresman, Inc. I remember the occasion of the letter's composition and mailing because it launched one of those "discussions" with my father in which he thought she should just let it alone, and she thought she shouldn't.

My mother was an inveterate letter writer — of complaints, congratulations, advice, travelogues, instructions, revelations, reminders, memory — it didn't matter; when the spirit moved her (and it did quite often), she wrote. Her letters gathered today would claim several volumes.

After she died I found letters she and my father had written to each other while both were students at Talladega College. During the summer separations, and especially after he had been called away from campus with most of the other male students for the war effort, he to join the Tuskegee division of black airmen, they wrote detailed, introspective, and loving letters to each other. What I call now her "Talladega series" is a fascinating set of letters, with rich and deeply provocative explanations of what she had been reading and what speakers had influenced her thought as well as the angst she felt over how her education was beginning to shift her views about religion. She wrote that she was concerned about how my grandparents might respond to her new determinations about religion.

I began to think at Talladega. Mine was the normal experience of one who had been raised in the traditional religious manner. I was alarmed and duly disturbed and I found myself easily throwing off some of the . . . ideas I had held, but others were neither primitive nor easy to discard. I became interested in philosophy . . . a whole new world opened up. I read Santayana. . . . I have ceased to believe that there are eternal verities. . . . This has landed me in the position of an eclectic. . . . I have come to look upon God . . . not as a spiritual being with omniscience and omnipotence, but as a center of values. . . . I heard Harry Emer-

son Fosdick and . . . Homer Kallen . . . I saw the very things that were
bothering me being treated in various ways by the world's greatest
thinkers. . . . Mom and Dad are shocked at my apparent change but
they have no idea to what extent it has gone. . . .

Ouida H. to Claude

Dec 12 1945

My older sister and I were the eventual legatees of that religious shift,
when, after our elementary school days, we left the African Methodist Episcopal church that we had been attending since birth and joined
the Unitarian Universalist church in Buffalo. We were just at the age
when we could appreciate and join the LRY (Liberal Religious Youth).
I remember these years with the Unitarian church as some of the best
Sundays of my youth—and they were enriched by the extraordinary
music of the choir, which Mother of course joined. Even today I can
recall the haunting strains of Mozart's "Lacrymosa" and the creative
play and fancy of Randall Thompson's *Frostiana*. From my perspective, hearing that choir and having the music I heard during those
years locate deep within my spirit were reason enough for Mother's
shift. It was an extra bonus to learn how well my listening to that
choir, and rehearsing its music with her at home, prepared me for the
demanding scores we would learn later as members of the Talladega
choir. The music of the Unitarian church on Ferry and Elmwood, and
its texts, then preached passionately by Reverend Paul Carnes, was
elegant, fine, diverse, and challenging. I treasure that time and am
grateful that our mother thought carefully enough about this to make
it possible. But I also know that this was not an easy decision. The letters from Talladega expressed her ambivalence about her shifting interests—and her parenting was always deeply rooted in cultural traditions. So this was a change that had to have been difficult for her
to make.

I think Mother waited until we were past fifth grade to make this
move not only because of her deep cultural loyalty to the traditions
of the African American church but because she wanted us to know
these well enough to understand the difference between the service

and philosophy of the two denominations. She believed that our early and culturally informed educations were both necessary and right, and that this time in a traditionally black church trumped her deeply political and intellectual interest in a Sunday sermon that would not form as familiar a text. But as soon as we were old enough to question some of what we heard, we joined the Unitarians. And when the Unitarian church in Buffalo declared its grounds a nuclear-free zone, I understood the difference that was her objective. It was my mother's interest in having a different exegesis inform our religious education. But she need not have worried that our cultural education would go lacking. Whenever our grandmother Celia got us to Detroit for the summer, she took care of mother's aberration by taking us straight to Saint Paul A.M.E. for Sunday, weekday, and evening services and programs. We made up for a lot of Buffalo Unitarianism in Detroit.

I imagine that mother may have written many a church member and preacher within the various denominations that marked the passages of her life during the eras of her membership. But the letter she wrote in the 1960s to the textbook publishing division of Scott Foresman had nothing to do with religion. It was about Tarzan.

My mother taught junior high school language arts before moving into school administration. As a language arts teacher, she was always hypercritical and cautious about the information she would share with her students from their textbooks. My mother was a race woman. Even though she had neither the stature nor the podium of an icon like Ida B. Wells or Anna Julia Cooper, she was intimately connected to that tradition. My mother was attentive, purposeful, and focused on matters of race and representation. So when she found that her language arts class textbook, assigned for the semester by "central administration," included a story about Tarzan by Edgar Rice Burroughs, she not only decided that she would eliminate it from her curriculum but decided that this culturally insensitive selection needed a response.

Tarzan was a book (or a selection from the book) in which "savage apes" and "savage men" were spoken of in the same breath and in which civilization and whiteness were equated and "the blacks" gratefully acknowledged and welcomed the new white jungle king as their superior. Given the lack of any other kind of black characters in these anthologies, and certainly none of its authors was black, my mother felt the images that were represented in the Tarzan selection were inaccurate, uninformed, and unacceptable and that she, for one, would not present this excerpt within the subjects she taught her students.

I have just a dim recollection of the letter itself. I've a much more vivid memory of my father wishing that she wouldn't take every oversight and cultural slight so personally—and plus, did she really think that a letter from her was going to make any difference whatsoever? Mother, as usual, prevailed, and off went her letter into what we all assumed was a no-where-land, or the recycling bins of the textbook mavens.

She never got a response that I knew of to the initial letter. Sometime in the early 1970s, however, an editor at Scott Foresman contacted her and said that they had kept her letter in a file these many years and that they were about to launch a major new textbook series, Medallion, and thought that she might agree to be one of its authors. She seemed not very surprised at all.

In the interim years between her letter and this response, the era of multiculturalism had dawned in public school classrooms, and the editors at Scott Foresman knew they needed representation from authors whose works were absent from their textbooks and advice from knowledgeable and informed professionals who could point them toward some "appropriate" literature. As a consequence of her letter, my mother was among the very first to select texts that would integrate the major school literary anthologies. The poetry, drama, and fiction sections of these books had not considered poems by Gwendolyn Brooks or short stories by Langston Hughes before the era when my mother joined the high school textbook editing world. After she reminded her three daughters of the value of an occasional epistle (she called it that—we were also raised to understand the absolute necessity of a "bread and butter note" and the art and value of

"Arrangement in Literature," 3 × 5 Medallion file cards/Medallion book.
Photo by Russell Holloway.

such a communication), she took on this task with an energy unlike any I had seen. And, as a home-from-college-for-the-summer English major, I was her gofer.

I had no idea about the complexity of a textbook selection process, the review of materials, the response cards to suggestions that each editor/author had to fill out, the decisions about use that included everything from its suitability to the audience, its copyright status, and whether it would fly in Texas or California—where the state education department made the textbook decisions for all school districts, and therefore the sales, if a book were adopted in these states, would be huge.

Recitation

My sisters Karen and Leslie and I grew up knowing the literature of black America, but our source was no book—it was our mother. She taught us "The Creation" from James Weldon Johnson's *God's Trombones.* We learned to enunciate with Langston Hughes's "The Negro Mother" and to linger with just-so-subtle shifts in emphasis over the repetitions in his "A Negro Speaks of Rivers." These pieces were not found in our school anthologies, but they were part of the corpus of materials that many black children learned for recitation in churches and Sunday schools—part of the outside-of-the-school cultural education that many parents took on as their responsibility to raise black children with some sense of the race. Historian John Hope Franklin's notes about his mother's teaching recall a similar education, as he remembers the way in which neither the text nor the impetus to improve on the school's curriculum in terms of "Negro" literature was an aberration:

> I had the example and the encouragement of both my parents. My mother no longer taught but she saw to it that my sister and I completed all of our home assignments promptly. Quite often, moreover, she introduced us to some of the great writers, especially Negro

authors, such as Paul Laurence Dunbar and James Weldon Johnson, who were not a part of our studies at school.[1]

Midcentury, the segregated schools of the South had black teachers, and in those schools, race literature was often shared, celebrated, and taught. One of the losses resulting from integrated schools in the South, other than the loss of black teachers who were deeply invested in children's potential, was the loss of that literature from the classroom. When Sonia Sanchez was asked about the influences on her writing, she remembers that she "used to read a lot of poetry. In the South we were given a lot of black poetry in school to memorize, mostly works by Paul Lawrence Dunbar and Langston Hughes."[2] Sanchez's memory implicitly draws attention to the difference between northern and southern schools. During the time of legally segregated schools in the South, black teachers taught from the culturally rich corpus that black northern parents like mine had to improvise. Sanchez's recollection echoes the history that Pauli Murray outlines in her autobiography, *Song in a Weary Throat*. Murray grew up in Durham, North Carolina, and her memory of what she read explains the shared values between home and school regarding the matter of books:

> Paul Laurence Dunbar was our favorite poet, both at home and in school. The 1907 edition of Dunbar's *Works* was the most worn book in our home library. My Aunt Roberta, who had died of typhoid fever before I was born, had used the title of his poem "Ships That Pass in the Night" as the theme of her high school graduation valedictory. His "Crust of Bread and a Corner to Sleep In," "Little Brown Baby with Sparklin' Eyes," and "Oh, Dere's Lot of Keer an' Trouble" were my bedtime nursery rhymes. At school, a child who could recite from memory "The Party" and "An Ante-Bellum Sermon" was in demand for all school programs.[3]

Murray makes a particular note of the ethic that emerges in this shared space of race literature, writing that in our segregated world, we had a sense of identity and a sense of racial pride, fragile though they might be. We were close to the roots of our immediate past because of the many elderly people still alive who had been born in slavery. To those of my generation reared in the South, it has always been somewhat bewildering to observe young blacks seeking an identity that we already had half a century earlier.

When libraries nurtured cultural inquiry and welcomed readers, there was a sanctuary that made memories of segregated library services especially poignant and sometimes painful. Sanchez recalls her move north and the librarian who stoked the interest and reinforced the cultural traditions that southern, black school teachers had introduced.

> When we moved north, I used to go to the library. The librarian would always see me moving around the poetry section. She was the one who turned me on to Langston Hughes and Gwen Brooks. She was the one who made me go back and examine the poets of the twenties and thirties. She also told me about Pushkin. One day this woman said to me, "This book is by a black man who lived in Russia." I read his poetry and just went crazy. I was twelve or thirteen.

It is important to understand that even after the Supreme Court's *Brown v. the Board of Education of Topeka* decision of 1954, southern black children whose schools refused to follow the federal mandate were initially still taught by black teachers. One of the consequences of the integration that eventually occurred is that when these children finally left segregated schools, many black teachers were either displaced or dispersed into formerly all-white schools. The lessons of culture and black tradition they had made central to their classes were left behind to echo through the emptied classrooms of their closed schools.

Sanchez's background mirrors the education my mother gave us out of school. Limited to the anthologies of the day, in which no

African American literati were represented, my mother made up the difference with us at home, in the way that Sanchez's southern teachers did at school and that the northern librarian continued. Sanchez also speaks to the issue of the high school anthologies that were in need of emendation:

> In high school I mostly read white writers. No one gave me any literary work by black writers to read. I did not get back to black writers until I got out of Hunter. That's a really terrible commentary on education. . . . I had been educated to think that Gwen Brooks and Langston Hughes were exceptions. In high school and college American Literature contained no black writers. As a consequence, the only time I saw "me" was in sociology courses, and then, I was an aberration.

Images of "me" for black children did matter. Sanchez's encounter with the famed Schomburg Library is nearly mystical in its import. It was an experience that led to her vision of herself as a writer:

> I went to the Schomburg Library. I'd just come from a job interview and got on the wrong train and got out at 135th Street and Lenox Avenue. It was hot, so I went inside to cool off. The librarian said that I couldn't take any books out. My response was, "What kind of library is this?" And she said that the books in there were by and for black people. I looked around and told her I didn't believe her. She gave me a personal tour. . . . I came back to that library for a week or two and I just read and read. I couldn't believe it. That's when I started buying books. I went down to 125th Street and met Mr. Michaux who owned a black bookstore. He told me what books to buy. I went back to the Schomburg and told the librarian that one day I'd have a book in there. I really meant it. I don't know what made me do that.

This was a library that mattered a great deal to children in Harlem, and memories of the place have found their way into more than one writer's memoir.

The 135th Street Branch Library, Harlem, during the 1950s. Photo courtesy of the Prints and Photograph Division, Schomberg Center for Research in Black Culture, New York Public Library, Astor, Lenox and Tilden Foundations.

Rather than the books she read there, it was the sanctuary of the space of the 135th Street library that Audre Lorde recalls. It was also the place where her mother lost the worry that her daughter was "tongue-tied" and would never speak. Lorde remembers that it was there, at the Harlem branch library, where she found the protection of a librarian, if not the library itself. The building that she recalls in her memoir is the Harlem library's first structure, before it was torn down "to make way for a new library building to house the Schomburg Collection on African-American History and Culture." She writes that she

> learned how to read from Mrs. Augusta Baker, the children's librarian at the old 135th Street branch library. . . . If that was the only good deed that lady ever did in her life, may she rest in peace. Because that deed saved my life, if not sooner, then later, when sometimes the only thing I had to hold on to was knowing I could read, and that that could get me through.[4]

That library was de facto sanctuary to Lorde. As Lorde tells it, her mother was fearful that her daughter's propensity for shrieking rather than speaking was a life-term malady, and she had few strategies that worked to keep her daughter from doing anything other than screaming. As a matter of fact, she had at least one that would assure this response:

> My mother was pinching my ear off one bright afternoon, while I lay spreadeagled on the floor of the Children's Room like a furious little brown toad, screaming bloody murder and embarrassing my mother to death. I know it must have been spring or early fall, because without the protection of a heavy coat, I can still feel the stinging soreness in the flesh of my upper arm. There, where my mother's sharp fingers had already tried to pinch me into silence. To escape those inexorable fingers I had hurled myself to the floor, roaring with pain as I could see them advancing toward my ears again. We were waiting to pick up my two older sisters from story hour, held upstairs on another floor

of the dry-smelling quiet library. My shrieks pierced the reverential stillness.

But Lorde recalls this moment as much for the torture as for the salvation. The association between her rescue and that librarian was a life-changing moment:

> suddenly, I looked up, and there was a library lady standing over me. My mother's hands had dropped to her sides. From the floor where I was lying, Mrs. Baker seemed like yet another mile-high woman about to do me in. She had immense, light, hooded eyes and a very quiet voice that said, not damnation for my noise, but "Would you like to hear a story, little girl?"

Lorde recalls that "by the time she had finished . . . I was sold on reading for the rest of my life" and that her mother's "surprised relief outweighed whatever annoyance she was still feeling at what she called my whelpish carryings-on."

Stories about Us

There is nothing in these comments about this moment in the library that particularizes them as an African American experience, except that they call attention to the famous landmark of the Harlem branch library. And were it not for the comments that precede these pages, it is a reading that would seem unmarked for race. But just a few pages prior to these, in her "biomythography" *Zami,* Lorde, like many African Americans of her generation, makes it clear that she marks her recollection of reading with her notice that she had no images of herself in schoolbooks. She writes that "all our storybooks were about people who were very different from us. They were blond and white and lived in houses with trees around and had dogs named Spot. I didn't know people like that any more than I knew people like Cinderella who lived in castles. Nobody wrote stories about us."

These kinds of memories—the search in a book for someone who looks like oneself or the dismay at not finding such an image—are part of a set of culturally explicit recollections from black readers, and we find the shared memories of these early readers emerging in the adult lives and professions of African Americans as different in occupation as author Toni Morrison and Olympic medalist Wilma Rudolph. Rudolph remembers "blotting out the pictures . . . and concentrating on the words" of her elementary school readers because "these books—See Dick Run, Watch Spot Run—[had] pictures of these white kids having happy times all the time."[5] Toni Morrison wrote of her memories of these books and of their impact on the story that would become her first novel, *The Bluest Eye*. She explained in the novel's afterword that writing the book was her effort to address the consequences of not seeing oneself as beautiful and of wishing for something so dramatically radical to a brown face (such as blue eyes) as a way of incorporating a gaze and a determination about beauty that have nothing to do with valuing one's own self. The novel begins with a passage from that early reader:

> Here is the house. It is green and white. It has a red door. It is very pretty. Here is the family. Mother, Father, Dick, and Jane live in the green-and-white house. They are very happy. See Jane. She has a red dress.

But Morrison destroys the coherence and the familiarity of the passage that schoolchildren around the nation discovered in their assigned early readers. These books were widely distributed—by the 1960s, 85 percent of public school students were being taught by these readers and pre-readers, published, ironically, by Scott Foresman.[6] Morrison takes the familiar text and corrupts it. It dissolves into a seamless and senseless passage that mirrors the loss of the book's main character, Pecola, the inchoate desire she has for someone other than herself, and the culpability of images that represent others and other families as worthwhile, and herself and her own as ugly.

> Hereisthehouseitisgreenandwhiteithasareddooritisveryprettyhereis
> thefamilymotherfatherdickandjaneliveinthegreenandwhitehousethey

areveryhappyseejaneshehasareddressshewantstoplaywhowillplaywith
janeseethecatitgoesmeowmeowcome.

In the 1954 *Brown v. the Board of Education* decision, which man-
dated integration of the nation's public schools, the Court cited the
research of psychologists Kenneth Bancroft Clark and Mamie Phipps
Clark. In the 1940s the Clarks had designed a test to determine what
psychological effects black children might experience as a result of
segregation. Kenneth Clark published the results in 1950, and they became part of the expert testimony heard in the lower court cases leading up to *Brown*. The Dick and Jane readers, used in more than half of
all U.S. schools by 1946, featured characters not unlike the white dolls
in the test that the Clarks performed in their research. In their famous
"doll test," using a white doll and black doll, they asked black schoolchildren which doll was nice and which one looked like them. African
American youngsters chose the white doll in both circumstances. For
those white Americans who might wonder about the significance of
looking for black images in schoolbooks or in the media, the doll test
is an important benchmark that indicates the potential consequences
to self-awareness and to self-esteem, as well as to stereotype. It visibly
argues the impact of schoolbooks like the Dick and Jane series on generations of black children, who see only images of white children with
happy families, and all of them presumably important enough to be
in a school textbook. Little wonder that Lorde looked for herself in the
illustrations in children's readers and that white children had no need
to consider whether their schoolbooks had stories that were about
anyone but perfect versions of themselves.

My mother's instinct in the 1960s was almost certainly informed by
Brown. But it was also, I suspect, deeply related to the education she
got as a youngster in Detroit. My grandmother would remind us to
"enunciate"—like no one else, except my mother. And I have heard
myself say this word to my own children, and to some of my students,
with particular care—as if, in saying it, the sense of how I wanted to
hear language spoken would be conveyed. I remember hearing it not

only during the times we practiced our recitations for declamation contests or church programs but in those instances of daily speech—how we were constantly reminded to put the medial *r* into a word central to this writing: *library*. "Enunciate . . . li-*bra*-ry," I was told on many an occasion.

When, a generation later, our ten-year-old Bem was robed in my master's gown with a kente-colored strip draping his shoulders, we watched with pride as he strode to our church lectern for an annual children's day presentation for Black History Month. He was to recite "The Creation." Each gesture rehearsed a legacy of instructions between families and across our generations. The dramatic pause between the title and the author's name, with each final syllable of "James" and "Weldon" and "Johnson" enunciated to the point of exaggeration. And then the step forward that I was taught and so taught him, to match the text "And God *stepped* out onto space." He was, at that moment, fully embraced within our family's traditions and the traditions of our race. I wonder today why I cannot hold that image, the resonance of his well-received text, or the amens and congratulations from the congregation, more securely in my memory; I long for that space of memory. But whatever my lacunae, I do know that Bem fulfilled, in that brief moment at least, his family's traditions in words.

We were careful, attentive, and focused on language in my family, and we expected language read or spoken to uplift and add to our confidence and self-assuredness. And if language or text were to offend, my mother's pen would be there, poised to write the requisite letter. Today it is likely that her letter would be interpreted as arguing for censorship, and quite frankly she was not above doing exactly that.

It was partially my mother's decision and on her advice that the junior high school literature book in the Medallion series that finally emerged from the editorial processes of Scott Foresman in 1979 would delete certain sections of Shakespeare's *Romeo and Juliet*—specifically those that suggested the hero and heroine's sexual intimacy. I have no doubt that the kinds of concerns that motivated her letter about the power and persuasion of the stereotyped characterizations in Tarzan, and the vulnerability of children (like those in the doll experiment) to embed those stereotypes, extended to her motherly concerns for her three daughters when she agreed to censor the sex in *Romeo and Juliet*. In that way our education, and that of the children in her classroom, which had prompted her letter to the publishers who thought Tarzan worthy for consumption by America's seventh and eighth graders, were much the same.

I worked all that summer with my mother, compiling and indexing those cards, discussing the potential impact of one of Gwendolyn Brooks's poems versus that of another for inclusion, having wonderful conversations about the things we held in common—a love of literature and its words. We thought up questions for the ends of the chapters, discussed what vocabulary might be challenging, composed lists of "additional readings" to suggest to instructors in the teacher's edition of these textbooks. The kitchen table was our workspace, and it was cluttered with index cards from a small metal file box—like the one a cook might use to keep recipes in. Cooking was neither my mother's interest nor her forte (we resemble each other here), so the kitchen table suffered no absence of attention from a cook's agenda. Instead it was a writing space, or studying space, or a paper-grading space, or during this very special summer, a book-writing space. But every once in a while, our mother would make the one dish that would earn our applause and kudos and make up for whatever absence she or we felt existed between her and the kitchen. It was lemon meringue pie. She taught us to use chilled water in a measuring cup with ice cubes to make the dough so that the pie's crust would turn out flaky. We watched with respect her fierce but disciplined whipping of egg whites until they turned into a glistening sheen of meringue, and she taught us how to add only part of the thick hot mixture of sugar and cornstarch that had come to a boil in the pan on the stove very quickly into the beaten egg yolks, and then to return that combination back to a low flame. It had turned a lemony yellow at that stage, as if to signal that we were close and that next we should add the lemon juice and the butter—stick butter back then. I always remembered what to do because I had organized the process by color—the white cornstarch, sugar, clear water; then the yellows. We

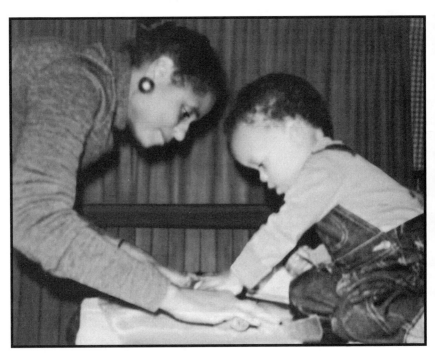

Ouida and her first grandchild Akili make a pie. Photo courtesy of the author.

learned to copy her stroke as she whipped the egg whites into stiff clouds that shimmered when they were ready for our final stage— to drop just enough vanilla flavoring but not enough to change the color. Mother's meringues always came out perfectly. There was a gentle brown just barely skimming the top of the meringue—just Karla's color and then it's done, Mommy used to say. And I thought how lovely to be meringue brown. There were always just a few tiny teardrops of golden sugar, or was it vanilla, "weeping" gently down the whipped peaks of pie. An appropriate response to this wonder our mother would bake. Whatever else she could not, or would not bake, broil, or grill, she made up for when she made lemon meringue pie. When her first grandchild was born, she put little Akili up on top of the kitchen table, where he knelt, Oshkosh overalls and all, roll- ing pie dough and learning to make lemon meringue pie from his grandmother. But in that summer of selecting readings for the new Scott Foresman anthology that would become its Medallion series, Mommy and I used that kitchen table in the best of a mother/daugh- ter and a cook's traditions. We stirred up combinations of words and books, sifted between authors, separated genres and generations, and finally emerged with a textbook that had a cultural flavor like none had ever had before that time. It was nearly better than pie.

4

A Prison Library

My reading had created a vast sense of distance between me and the world in which I lived.

RICHARD WRIGHT, *Black Boy*

I N 1998, the Directors' Review Committee of the Texas prison system banned Toni Morrison's newly published novel *Paradise* from Texas prisons because it contained "information of a racial nature" that "a reasonable person would construe as written solely for the purpose of communicating information designed to achieve a breakdown of prisons through inmate disruption, such as strikes or riots." [1] The first line of *Paradise* is "They killed the white girl first." Although that line might certainly seem provocative and a signal of the novel's purpose and plan, anyone who read *Paradise* would not place the work into the category that provoked the review committee's decision. I remember the academic world's shock, outrage, and surprise at this determination. It seemed that many of my colleagues had been unaware that these kinds of judgments were happening all the time, in states across the country. Their righteous indignation and disdain had not much impact on that decision, and as far as I can tell, the outrage itself had a rather abbreviated life as a subject of conversation even within the academy. It certainly did not provoke any change in prison policies. Prisoners in North Carolina, and this may be true of other states as well, cannot receive any books at all from individuals —only directly through publishers. And the prison's guards or committees censor them as well—bringing who knows what standards or even acumen to the process. Do they decide yes or no on the basis of a title? An apparent "racial nature"? The first line? The rest of the text? Do they read any of the books themselves? It's a mystery and an irritant that I never spent much time worrying over. I was too occupied with selecting books that I could send to the prison that incarcerated our son. I mailed them to my generous-beyond-measure friend L, who took the books I bundled up and forwarded to her, generously repackaged them into the official boxes or envelopes of her profession, and forwarded without any other comment but this expression of care for us to our son in prison.

I sent Orson Scott Card's *Ender's Game* and Marian Wright Edelman's *The Measure of Our Success: A Letter to My Children and Yours.* I sent Tolkien and *Gifted Hands,* the autobiography of Ben Carson, and I sent the book of Psalms from his grandmother, and books that I will never retrieve, much less remember. But I do recall the visit during which he told me he had finally read *Ender's Game,* a book I had been urging on him since early adolescence. He said I was right about it being so absorbing that he almost could not put it down once he got into it. I smiled with a satisfaction I rarely had on those visits. I think I even talked to him about Ender and his friend and the way in which the game turns out to be the real thing. We chatted happily, and I know he felt happy that he had made me feel that I had sent him something he appreciated, and that he was finally reading. There were no matchbox cars to choose instead. We were far past that moment of youth, and choice. But maybe, and hopefully, I thought, he could yet find a sanctuary in reading. I know that I wanted, and desperately needed, to believe that he'd be left alone if he was reading, that it would occupy him and separate him, and that these books could be both an escape and a protection. I was fooling myself.

It is an irony now that I don't even like to recall—that in our home, while the children were growing up, the rule was that you could never disturb a reader. If there was a book in their hands, they were free from running errands, or setting the table, or any of the little tasks and annoyances that parents can think of to give children a sense of their responsibility in the house. Ayana usually had a book. Bem didn't. So you know who got saddled with the annoyances. But then a terrible series of years came to us when our parenting was reduced to selecting books to send to him in prison, with the hope that some of the hours and days and events would be mediated, even erased, as he placed his mind into the world of a book rather than into the horror of the miserable space around him. The irony of responsibility and reality, as measured against Bem's childhood and his adolescence and brief young adulthood, was sometimes difficult to hold, much less to believe was ours to negotiate.

Reading Privileges

That black men and boys especially have stories that emerge from reading in prison is an unsurprising dimension of the African American experience. Given the historically consistent patterns of incarceration of this population in the United States, their disappearance to prison is familiar enough to too many African American families. Rituals and patterns of response to these incarcerations have emerged, and are shared, including ways of sending books past the bureaucracies of guards, who have little credible facility of discernment. Black literature has relied on the sign of a prison space to convey a story too thick to tell. James Baldwin's semi-autobiographical *Go Tell It on the Mountain* recalls that, while he was growing up in the middle of Harlem, his mother thought the only destination for her sons might be jail or church, and she struggled to make certain it was the latter.

Eldridge Cleaver, writing in *Soul on Ice* of his own incarceration in Folsom State Prison, talks in detail about the importance of books. In his chapter "A Day in Folsom Prison," he rants about the prison's book-related procedures: "talk about hypocrisy: you should see the library. We are allowed to order, from the state library, only nonfiction and law books. Of the law books, we can only order books containing court opinion. . . . But books of an explanatory nature are prohibited."[2]

Cleaver is only eighteen at the time of his incarceration for marijuana possession, but he uses this autobiographical moment to claim that he had an idea of what literature he would have wanted available to him had the library not had those regulations. But he also says he can't devote time to reading and writing in prison because he has "to keep my eyes open at all times, or I won't make it."

Soul is nevertheless a memoir that, in the tradition of black letters, falls into the pattern of booklists. In Cleaver's narrative he remarks on the books he read as well as on those he would have wanted to read. His comments manage an inverted acknowledgment of the tradition: "I've been dying to read Norman Mailer's *An American Dream,* but that too is prohibited." The statement indicates his capacity to discern among authors, marking those who would fall into the same category of the wish list that Mailer's novel allows him to introduce. Cleaver writes what is effectively a critique of the library's collection:

> The library does have a selection of very solid material, things done from ten years ago all the way back to the Bible. But it is unsatisfactory to a stud who is trying to function in the last half of the twentieth century. Go down there and try to find Hemingway, Mailer, Camus, Sartre, Baldwin, Henry Miller, Terry Southern, Julian Mayfield, Bellow, William Burroughs, Allen Ginsberg, Herbert Gold, Robert Glover, J. O. Killens, etc.—no action.

Cleaver's complaint that the prison's rules automatically eliminate books that are about black folk is obviously disingenuous. It seems his objective is actually to inform his reader about something essential to his own intellectual capability through the familiarity he can claim regarding certain kinds of books. He uses for his critique about "automatic elimination of black subjects" a book that reports on a North Carolina community that armed itself to fight back against Klan violence directed toward them, and on the man who led this resistance. Cleaver gives only the title of the volume, not even acknowledging that the book likely would be considered a provocation, given his surroundings. Without an explanation of its content, his reader is likely to take at face value his point that this was a reasonable book to make available to the prison population. But if we know the contents of the book, it seems reasonable to suspect that prison authorities might have concerns about its circulation in the prison population. Cleaver writes that "the system also has this sick thing going when it comes to books by and about Negroes. Robert F. Williams' book, *Negroes with Guns*, is not allowed anymore. I ordered it from the state library before it was too popular around here. I devoured it and let a few friends read it, before the librarian dug it and put it on the blacklist."

What Cleaver does manage to accomplish here, however, is important in the tradition of the bookmark. He uses the occasion of a list to distinguish himself from the rest of the population—*he* had

The Folsom Prison Library was located in the trailer behind the large tower. In 1971 the Supreme Court, in Gilmore v. Lynch, *ruled that prisoners must have access to libraries and law books. Folsom was one of the last prisons to comply. Photo courtesy of the Folsom Prison Museum.*

ordered the book, and *he* had shared it. The book selection he uses here as if to comment on the library's censorship of black writers instead allows him to mark the revolutionary sensibility he might claim through his inspired ordering of a book on such a topic. His mention of it here, and subsequently, functions in exactly the way that bookmarks operate in the rest of the African American tradition—as a sign of a certain kind of readerly acumen and vision.

Cleaver's need to distinguish himself here is somewhat more poignant, however. His lack of choice and freedom and the way in which he has been pulled into the mass identity of "prisoner" makes his loss and need that much more articulated. John Wideman, writing in *Brothers and Keepers* of his brother's imprisonment and their shared decision to write about his incarceration, attempts both to mediate the horror and to reach toward that same urge of distinction. Wideman too is left with language read or spoken or written to manage this loss. In the following passage, he makes apparent what the incarcerated and those who love them look for in this reach toward words:

> I'd ask Robby to write out a schedule of a typical day. . . . When were the mealtimes, work times, free periods in the yard? Was it like high school? Did bells or P.A. announcements punctuate the prison day? Were all the lights in the range extinguished at a certain hour or were prisoners allowed reading privileges in their cells? I needed that kind of concrete, mundane information so I could walk through a day with Robby on paper.[3]

The order of literacy's form and structure, and its organization of space—and even displacement of space—seem the extent of reach of those within and without these jailhouses. But each used what might be gained from text differently, depending on whether it was something a parent or a brother expressed, or something that an inmate constructed.

Malcolm X's autobiography is the book that is familiar to many Americans, and one that easily fits into the traditions of bookmarks. It certainly influenced my own desires regarding my son's prison reading. Might he emerge with a similar conversion experience? Isn't this autobiography one way to consider a good ending, or at least a better one, to a moment that seemed headed for the tragedy that eventually did engulf and claim him and us?

Malcolm X credits prison with being the space where reading began to matter to him, and the passionate and fully engaged language that he used to characterize both the habit of reading in prison and its consequence was something I imagined as possible for my son as well. I latched onto a prison reading plan that I would assure by getting him books any way that I could. Malcolm X wrote of the kind of transformation I wished for:

> Anyone who has read a great deal can imagine the new world that opened. Let me tell you something: from then until I left that prison, in every free moment I had, if I was not reading in the library, I was reading on my bunk. You couldn't have gotten me out of books with a wedge. . . . [With] my reading of books, months passed without my even thinking about being imprisoned.
>
> In fact, up to then, I never had been so truly free in my life.[4]

For him, the library space itself was neither hostile nor restricted. In fact, he writes with some admiration of its collection and speaks of the uses to which the library was put in a way that fully associates his appreciation with having taken advantage of a certain quality of services represented in the depth of the collection, the schooling of those who came to teach, and the way in which the collection was suitable for a college.

> The Norfolk Prison Colony's library was in the school building. A variety of classes was taught there by instructors who came from such places as Harvard and Boston universities. . . . Available on the prison library's shelves were books on just about every general subject. Much of the big private collection that Parkhurst had willed to the prison was still in crates and boxes—thousands of old books. Some of them looked ancient: covers faded, old-time parchment-looking binding.

Parkhurst . . . seemed to have been principally interested in history and religion. He had the money and the special interest to have a lot of books that you wouldn't have in general circulation. Any college library would have been lucky to get that collection.

Malcolm X establishes his "nearness" and his intimacy with those books, the library, and the college-level quality of its presence as a way of indicating that he might share their credibility, or at least that it might be passed on to him—and that there were ways the associations between those books and his body would have made him distinct in that company of inmates. These were, after all, books of such value that they would not have been in "general circulation." He continues to emphasize the distinctiveness that he earned and practiced through books:

> I read more in my room than in the library itself. An inmate who was known to read a lot could check out more than the permitted maximum number of books. I preferred reading in the total isolation of my own room. When I had progressed to really serious reading . . . when "lights out" came, I would sit on the floor where I could continue reading in the glow [of the corridor light].

When Wideman's brother Robby writes of reading in his cell, we also understand the contradictions and complications of this space, and the displacement that Malcolm had to achieve to positively reconstruct that space as a reading opportunity rather than the challenge that Robby Wideman helps us to understand: "You in your own cell, and can't see nobody else. Barely enough light to read by . . . it feels like being alone so much . . . it feels like you're singing or reading to somebody else."

The ways that prison spaces are negotiated around reading and books is engaged in a similar way in Claude Brown's *Manchild in the Promised Land.* Even though he is not in prison but in a detention home when he finds this sanctuary, his story resonates with that of Malcolm X, Robby Wideman, and Eldridge Cleaver through the way

in which the space of incarceration is renegotiated with books. Brown
writes that

> most of the time, I used to just sit around in the cottage reading. I didn't
> bother with people, and nobody bothered me. This was a way to be
> in Warwick and not to be there at the same time. I could get lost in a
> book. Cats would come up and say "Brown, what you readin'?" and I'd
> just say, "Man git the fuck on away from me, and don't bother me." [5]

Angela Davis, in a singular commentary on reading and prison
written by an African American woman in this tradition of bookmarks, writes against the trend of using books as an escape in a critique that testifies to the focused politics of both her incarceration
and her professional life. The library collection in the Women's Detention Center in New York failed her interests, specifically because it
appealed to those who may have wanted to use books as a diversion
from the prison's physical confinement. Davis writes that "for those
who enjoyed reading, the library would have been a saving grace had
it not been for the fact that the vast majority of the books were mysteries, romances and just plain bad literature whose sole function was
to create emotional paths of escape." She found only "a few books
which held the slightest interest; a book on the Chinese Revolution
by Edgar Snow, the autobiography of W.E.B. Du Bois and a book on
communism written by an astonishingly objective little-known author." In a process not unlike Malcolm X's, Davis indicates here her interest in using the prison library to sustain a political education, but at
the same time she is forwarding a critical review of the library's hold-
ings. She also remarks on the processes of prisons with regard to books
and shows generosity and an interest in her fellow inmates' reading
materials—an interest that is considerably less self-congratulatory
than Cleaver's and with a bureaucratic oversight that I remember
as well:

> If you wanted books which were not in the library, they had to be
> mailed directly from the publisher. I decided to have as many books

sent to me as possible, so as to provide, for succeeding prisoners, literature that was more interesting, more relevant, more serious than the trash on the shelves of the library. Apparently, the jailers saw through my scheme, especially when ten copies of George Jackson's *Soledad Brother* came in, for they harshly informed me that none of my books were to leave my hands. They would follow me to whichever jail I went.[6]

There is some reverie in these notes about prisons and books, but Davis, Malcolm X, and Cleaver emphasize that prison libraries are serious and sustained spaces for gathering information and gaining an education. Davis makes it absolutely clear that she saw the prison library as a space for her political education as well as the space that allowed for a defining moment in her political identity and legacy:

After my discovery of these books, my thoughts kept wandering back to their enigmatic presence. And suddenly it hit me: they had probably been read by Elizabeth Gurley Flynn, Claudia Jones or one of the other Communist leaders who had been persecuted under the Smith Act during the McCarthy era. I myself had been told that if I received any books during my time there, I would have to donate them to the library—which was a pleasure, considering the state of that so-called place of learning. As I turned the pages of those books, I felt honored to be following in the tradition of some of this country's most outstanding heroines: Communist women leaders, especially the Black Communist Claudia Jones.

For Malcolm X the prison library was a space of transformation. He spends a good deal of time in his autobiography introducing and explaining his personal evolution, and indeed the reconstruction of the man he was to become. Books were critical to this enterprise and stood in place of a formal education. His booklist made apparent that even without that formality, his experience was selective and especially erudite. When he does eventually turn to the actual books he read, they reinforce this persona, emphasizing a mix of commentary,

review, and response not unlike those bookmarks in the tradition
from writers with more formally accomplished backgrounds:

> I can remember accurately the very first set of books that really im-
> pressed me. I have since bought that set of books and have it at home
> for my children to read as they grow up. It's called *Wonders of the World*.
> It's full of pictures of archeological finds . . . that depict, usually, non-
> European people. I found books like Will Durant's *Story of Civiliza-
> tion*. I read H. G. Wells' *Outline of History*. *Souls of Black Folk* by W.E.B.
> Du Bois gave me a glimpse into the Black people's history before they
> came to this country. Carter G. Woodson's *Negro History* opened my
> eyes about black empires before the black slave was brought to the
> United States, and the early Negro struggles for freedom. J. A. Rog-
> ers's three volumes of sex and race told me about race-mixing before
> Christ's time: about Aesop's being a black man who told fables; about
> Egypt's Pharaohs; about the great Coptic Christian Empires; about
> Ethiopia, the earth's oldest continuous black civilization.

One cannot help but read his commentary here as a kind of evidence
—a report that testifies to the fact that he not only knows the titles
but he knows what these books are about, speaking back to a potential reader's doubt of his accomplishment. He is careful to pronounce
this list within the developing awareness of his faith and the politics of
the Black Muslim movement, which would credit Elijah Muhammad
as the substance and source of all interests and teaching. Malcolm X
notes, for example, that "Mr. Muhammad's teaching about how the
white man had been created led me to *Findings in Genetics* by Gregor
Mendel."

Malcolm X's list additionally places him in a position where he can
knowledgably comment on the history of black folk—and he extends
his "book reporting" when it comes to the histories of slavery to what
seem to be instructions to the reader on how to understand these
texts. He is cautious and circumspect enough to make clear whether
he was reading the work of a historical figure or reading about him.
His list evidences an effort to make it credible and reliable. And it is

interesting that rather than saying he was reading books in the prison library, he makes the prison space disappear and replaces it with the philanthropist's name:

> Books like the one by Frederick Olmsted opened my eyes to the hor-
> rors suffered when the slave was landed in the United States. The Eu-
> ropean woman, Fannie Kimball, who had married a Southern white
> slaveowner, described how human beings were degraded. Of course I
> read *Uncle Tom's Cabin.* . . . I believe that's the only novel I have ever
> read since I started serious reading. Parkhurst's collection also con-
> tained some bound pamphlets of the Abolitionist Anti-Slavery Society
> of New England. I read descriptions of atrocities, saw those illustra-
> tions. . . . I read about the slave preacher Nat Turner, who put the fear
> of God into the white slavemaster. . . . I read Herodotus, the "father of
> History," or, rather, I read about him. And I read the histories of vari-
> ous nations. . . . I remember, for instance, books such as Will Durant's
> story of Oriental civilization, and Mahatma Gandhi's accounts of the
> struggle to drive the British out of India.

Malcolm X's litany of books is among the most impressive specifically because it contains references to world literature and culture outside of European or British traditions. We see this interest reflected in his later life, when he travels to Mecca, and this journey concludes with a life-altering change in philosophy. His effort to impress on his read-ers the list's credibility and his own is more pronounced. It must ac-complish a different kind of extrication from place and space than for other writers who write with race as their potential hurdle. Malcolm X's identity must be doubly distanced. So his effort to make the list credible to his readers goes further than other writers. He writes with a presumptive awareness that he might need to earn his reader's cred-ibility and that one way to do so would be to displace the environs of a prison's library with what stands in the place of a formal education. I suspect that in this narrative his moving his reading from that library to his cell accomplishes that distance for him, as does his renaming the source of his books the Parkhurst collection rather than calling it the prison library. One nearly forgets that the collection is an endowment to a prison library. His attentive awareness of audience is like that of other writers in the tradition, but Malcolm X seems to shape his narrative with more deliberate attention as to how his readers might respond than do the others. We know he comes away from that prison experience with a deeply informed judgment about public presentation, style, and narrative—exactly the kinds of gifts that reading offers. I reread Malcolm's autobiography at that time of horror in my life to convince myself again that someone like our son might emerge from that experience as a cautious and circumspect thinker, and to give me some hope that he might be safe. I should have considered then the end of Malcolm's days as the rest of that text.

Of course some promise or potential of self-improvement, contemplation, and appreciation of the notion that there were worlds beyond the walls of a prison was what I hoped would be the residue of my son's experience. I longed for that assured and informed and thoughtful view of the world and its histories and its mysteries as the consequence of my son's prison reading and even his inspiration. But one day, near the end, in a kind of confessional as I see it now, he told me, Mom, you know I never really read that book *Ender's Game*. I couldn't reply. I was remembering sharing that conversation with him, sharing a knowing smile about how good the book was, being drawn into participating, once again and unwittingly, in one of his fantasies, or lies. But then he said, I just knew it would make you happy to think I did, and I wanted so much for you to be happy. You come to see me so sad all the time, I thought that might be something I could say to change how you felt.

Bittersweet. How else do I think about that loving gesture that indicated there would be no sanctuary for him in books, no imagination prompted from those pages, no desire shaped and then sought after? But it meant as well that he loved me enough to want my happiness, that there was some ache in him seeing what we had become after losing him to a prison and its terrors, and that he chose exactly the thing, or the only thing he had that might indeed make me happy, even in the midst of our losing him.

Some time after that I sent him a note on one of those blank-inside cards you can find at a bookstore. The image on the front of the card was from Maurice Sendak's *Where the Wild Things Are.* No, I did not mean to signify with that card—and he knew it. He told me, I loved that letter. It made me smile. It reminded me of your reading that book to us.

And there I had it—that bookish moment of intimacy and desire, if only in a memory, that I could share with him. And for that instant, it was enough.

5

The Anchor Bar

*And if my eyes conceal a squadron of conflicting rebellions, I learned
from you to define myself through your denials.*

Audre Lorde, "Black Mother Woman"

I PAUSED when I read Malcolm X's almost parenthetical aside that *Uncle Tom's Cabin* was the only fiction he ever read. Something in it—the claim and the assertion of the vaulted place of nonfiction in his reading—reminded me of my father. I can hear him now impatiently asking why didn't we ever read nonfiction. Asserting the privilege of nonfiction over the imaginary, he urged us to please put away the novels and read some biography. "Why don't you read some history?" he would plead. Had he known about the comic books under the bed, he'd have begun that supplication to his daughters from a far different perspective.

Actually, the only reason we hid the comic books was that we knew that if fiction was a problem for him, these would make him tremendously disappointed. We knew he thought this absolutely unsuitable reading for girls who would one day become members of the educated elite. My father was a serious, deeply loving, and private man. He was extraordinarily careful with his daughters, and he encouraged us through both the example of his own integrity and his demeanor. His quiet and calm were the opposite of my mother's energy and socially engaged spirit. Today, I discover more in me like my father than my mother. His aspirations and expectations for his daughters were paramount in his advice to us, as were his preferences. We absolutely wanted his pride and approval—but we also wanted to read Wonder Woman.

The boy down the block, just seven houses away from ours, kept my sister Karen and me in good supply of just-read-once comic books. John could buy them with impunity, and he would generously pass them on to us as soon as he finished. Our only problem was what to do with them after that. So under our bed was a stash of comic books: Superman, Supergirl—the whole lot of "nonsense" that my father would have found totally distressing. Had he only known about the parents of daughters who would turn out to be poet laureates, daughters like Rita Dove, he may have been more flexible. Rita Dove recalled that her parents "let us read comics. Their philosophy was that you could read anything. If you wanted to read it, you could read it. If we understood it, fine. If we didn't, well, we'd stop. I think that was wise because I loved comic books for a while, but later I outgrew them. I really did grow up on Wonder Woman and Superman and all those super American heroes." [1]

Actually, knowing about these parents and their soon-to-be-poet-laureate daughter would not have moved my father "one iota" (his favorite descriptor) away from his position. Both my parents were masters of the "just because it is done in someone else's family" mantra. Nevertheless, despite my father's preference, and in addition to those colorful passions for the comic book, we were also avid readers of fiction. And since there was no stash of fiction to be found in my father's den among the serious and exemplary collection of histories and biography, we found our fictions in the downtown library. An indication of my parents' sense of the importance of this institution and the value they assigned to our reading, as well as their trust in us (however misplaced it may have been, given the evidence of the stash of comics), was that it was the only trip we were allowed to make by ourselves. On this, my parents would have found agreement with Rita Dove's. Dove recalled that "one place we could always go (assuming it wasn't storming or sleeting) was the library. Of course, we could always abuse that privilege: 'I'm going to the library,' and then I'd make a little side trip, but we did go to the library because we had to bring books back."

My bus money was given with its explicit association between it and the library. And I made no side trips. Saturday mornings reliably and eagerly found me at the stop on the corner of Main Street and Virginia in Buffalo, waiting for the bus that would take me downtown. I walked farther to that stop than anywhere else in my childhood, even to school, and I cherished each moment of the private space it gave me, the chance for uninterrupted reverie that would be reinforced as soon as I got to the library. Being rather directionally challenged then, as I still am today, I relied on landmarks to make certain I had not veered from my course.

My landmark for the corner where the bus would transport me downtown was the famed Anchor Bar, whose chicken ("Buffalo") wings have legendary status in Buffalo and its environs. I actually did not go inside the Anchor Bar until I was an adult and had returned to Buffalo with my husband, who had heard of the chicken wings and whose appetite for the renowned and messy delicacy urged me into the small restaurant for what would become the first of many adult orders. As a youngster, however, the Anchor Bar was a just a landmark to wonder at. I don't believe I even knew about its chicken wings until I had left for college, where people who found I was from Buffalo asked me about the Anchor Bar. I remember it as my place mark, waiting for the bus and wondering who might venture into a bar so early in a morning—whose craving for liquor might need to be satisfied as early as my trip to the library. I did not know it as a restaurant; I took the "Bar" in its name quite literally. My mother had signed a temperance pledge as a child, it's there in our family Bible, and as far as I know she not only never broke it but occasionally launched into a lecture about the tragedy of alcohol and all those who drank it. There was balance in my household. I could eat the cherries from my father's Manhattans, and I had my first drink of wine with him—although to his dismay, when I ordered Manischewitz in the restaurant he took me to, he grimaced and changed my order to something that befit the class he thought he had introduced me into.

But every Saturday I crossed the street when I got to the Anchor Bar and waited for the No. 5 bus to take me down to the library, where I got more of the works of fiction that my father continued to complain were not suitable background for my training. I don't know what career he imagined for me then. Years later, when my interest in biography and history became nearly insatiable, I thought back to those early days on the street corner of Main and Virginia waiting for the bus and watching to see who might venture into the Anchor Bar, and wondered why I had waited until so late to read books like the ones that had waited for me so patiently in my father's den.

Negotiating Reading and Race

My sisters' and my reading choices were often a negotiation between parents and teachers, who had one vision of our potential, and ourselves, who had practically none—or who, like Maya Angelou, had an interest in marking her difference from her mother's desire. Angelou writes about her reading in the first of her several autobiographies—*I Know Why the Caged Bird Sings,* the most widely known and recognized of the collection. Especially interesting in her booklist is the way it appears to negotiate between two traditions—one black and the other white—so that she successfully manages to effectively claim knowledge and familiarity with them both. She not only takes the first autobiography's title from a hallmark piece of black literature, Paul Lawrence Dunbar's poem, but she finds a way to at least a nod toward the tradition of black writers. Two traditions emerge in her telling, but her intimacy and desire are reserved for the classics, and it is these works that Angelou wants to make certain her reader understands are fully within her grasp. It is a claim that seems to match the adult Angelou, who, in annual presentations to the new class of Duke University undergraduates, always manages to let her audience know how thoroughly literate she is. Her most consistent approach to the subject of her background is to reveal to the gathered first-year students that she can speak five (or perhaps it is six) languages. She does this by greeting the students in each of the languages from her repertoire. Testimony, it appears, to the ways in which her education is broad and deep. Those who have heard "the speech" on more than one occasion note its consistency, especially this dimension of the presentation. It arguably indicates that it is important to the adult Angelou to shape the audience's understanding and reception of her. But it also seems connected to a strategy similar to the framing of her childhood in the first autobiography, wherein she constructs an image that leaves no question for her readers that she has been sufficiently informed by and impressed with African American literary traditions. This message is inescapable, but even as she makes this point clear, we learn that her "love" of the classics also mattered deeply to her.

> During these years in Stamps, I met and fell in love with William Shakespeare. He was my first white love. Although I enjoyed and respected Kipling, Poe, Butler, Thackeray and Henley, I saved my young and loyal passion for Paul Lawrence Dunbar, Langston Hughes, James

Weldon Johnson and W.E.B. Du Bois' "Litany at Atlanta." But it was Shakespeare who said, "When in disgrace with fortune and men's eyes." It was a state with which I felt myself most familiar. I pacified myself about his whiteness by saying that after all he had been dead so long it couldn't matter to anyone any more.[2]

Angelou's classic rhetorical strategy here, to make both claim and disclaimer simultaneously, is beautifully executed. She not only manages to mark certain respected and well-recognized names in two literary traditions, but she does so in a manner that introduces a subtle but nonetheless essential distinction.

The difference of "being in love" and having a "young and loyal passion for" is a distinction that seems to rest between a designation of something formal rather than informal, controlled rather than disorderly. In this divide, she makes a subtle but telling commentary marking what might arguably be her hierarchies within literary traditions.

Yet another indication of this implicit hierarchy is the way in which she devotes her effort to marking a booklist subtly balanced toward white authors, and especially Shakespeare. I might be overreading here, but I think my interpretation of where she wants her readers to believe her preferences and expertise lie is validated when we look more closely at the rest of the Shakespearean text from which she selects her illustration. The sonnet is abbreviated in *Caged Bird,* where she cites only the first lines, but the entire sonnet 29 reveals a bit more about her choice and her desire:

> When in disgrace with fortune and men's eyes
> I all alone beweep my outcast state,
> And trouble deaf heaven with my bootless cries,
> And look upon myself, and curse my fate,
> Wishing me like to one more rich in hope,
> Featured like him, like him with friends possessed,
> Desiring this man's art, and that man's scope,
> With what I most enjoy contented least;

Yet in these thoughts my self almost despising,
Haply I think on thee, and then my state,
Like to the lark at break of day arising
From sullen earth, sings hymns at heaven's gate;
For thy sweet love remembered such wealth brings
That then I scorn to change my state with kings.

It is Angelou who has placed these lines into a racialized context, asserting Shakespeare's whiteness and making it matter in her discussion here. It is therefore difficult to read these lines as something other than her own longing to be "like one more rich in hope/Featured like him . . . Desiring this man's art." It is helpful as well to recall, with this citation, the way that literature, desire, and intimacy interact and to better understand her strategic declamation that this author was her "*first* white love"—making plain to her reader that intimacy with the racial other is neither outside her experience, nor her desire. In this context, the sonnet reads even more deeply into the strategic selectivity of her booklist.

Like many black youngsters whose childhood occasioned recitations and public addresses, Angelou places herself and her brother into that important oral tradition. She doesn't reveal the occasion (if there is one); it seems in this writing merely a childhood recreation that siblings chose during some playtime moment: "Bailey and I decided to memorize a scene from 'The Merchant of Venice,' but we realized that Momma would question us about the author and we'd have to tell her that Shakespeare was white, and it wouldn't matter to her whether he was dead or not. So we chose 'The Creation' by James Weldon Johnson instead." Her failure to name the occasion of this recitation or dramatic play allows her to leave the impetus for the memorization unclear and to further distinguish the quality of her childhood play (how many children choose to memorize a scene from Shakespeare for their playtime activity?) even while it claims some relation—however distanced—to the folk. So we don't know whether the occasion here comes from a childhood game or a performance for church or school.

For black schoolchildren in the South, recitation was a traditional part of the curriculum, and for these children James Weldon Johnson's "The Creation" was a popular text. Angelou makes her reader aware that she too participated in that tradition, even though she had in her repertoire a scene from Shakespeare's *The Merchant of Venice*. But at the same time she manages to place into the record that her first instinct and wish was a scene from Shakespeare, emphasizing again the way in which she balances her access to and difference from a black literary tradition. Other references to books in this autobiography follow, with her marking the readings of books and authors that would be labeled classics. When writing reflectively about the impact of her early years on her adult life, she again makes clear the works that best capture, or most resemble, her spirit and imagination, and those she had already selected to read on her own, before a parent or teacher made a suggestion for her.

An autobiographical essay by scholar bell hooks reflects an interest in books that is similar to Angelou's. But the differences help illustrate the particular focus of Angelou's memories regarding books and authors. Hooks also writes about the importance of reading, and the escape it provided her, in an essay shifting between the voices of the first and third person. For example, when she writes about the traditions of straightening hair with a hot comb in her family, it is in a first-person voice that she writes, "I cannot participate in the ritual. I have good hair that does not need pressing." [3] She writes about reading using the third person, perhaps as a way of avoiding the "conventional," which she notes in the passage that follows. Hooks's embrace of the Romantic tradition, like Angelou's, seems to follow a model in which a traditional, or classic, literature matters greatly to her adolescent desire. It is also a world that separates and arguably distinguishes her from the adults in her community. Both Angelou and hooks indicate this difference, with hooks writing that "she wants to express herself —to speak her mind. To them it is just talking back." But in the distinction hooks makes between her parents and others in her community, even with the distance of her third-person voice and the embrace of "another world" that she finds in books, she does not set black and white traditions into the implicit competition that Angelou embraces:

> When she discovers the Romantics it is like losing a part of herself and recovering it. She reads them night and day, all the time. She memorizes poems. She recites them while ironing or washing dishes. Reading Emily Dickinson she senses that the spirit can grow in the solitary life. She reads Edna St. Vincent Millay's "Renascence," and she feels with the lines the suppression of spirit, the spiritual death, and the longing to live again. She reads Whitman, Wordsworth, Coleridge. Whitman shows her that language, like the human spirit, need not be trapped in conventional form or traditions. For school she recites "O Captain, My Captain." She would rather recite from *Song of Myself* but they do not read it in school.

The brief parallels between hooks and Angelou illustrate the way in which Angelou seems to labor over securing an implicit relationship between her intellectual acumen and a certain literature. In a style that recalls the final claim of Douglass's *Narrative*—written by "himself," Angelou writes to directly associate these authors and her reading with her body. Her booklists seem more than annotation; they read as documentation. When Mrs. Flowers, the teacher and neighbor who inspires her love and appreciation for recitation, invites her to her home and reads to her from a Dickens classic, Angelou is generous in the credit to Mrs. Flowers for the inspiration that might follow from the spoken word, but she maintains as well enough authority to let her reader know that she had already read the book.

> I had read *A Tale of Two Cities* and found it up to my standards as a romantic novel. She opened the first page and I heard poetry for the first time in my life. "It was the best of times and the worst of times." Her voice slid in and curved down over the words. She was nearly singing. I wanted to look at the pages. Were they the same that I had read?

When Mrs. Flowers gives her a book of poems and asks Angelou to recite for her the next time, Angelou reflects on this moment, recalling other names from literature, and in a passage echoing the ease with which Du Bois placed himself into the company of an elite literary group, Angelou writes:

> I have tried often to search behind the sophistication of years for the enchantment I so easily found in those gifts. The essence escapes but its aura remains. To be allowed, no, invited, into the private lives of strangers, and to share their joys and fears, was a chance to exchange the Southern bitter wormwood for a cup of mead with Beowulf or a hot cup of tea and milk with Oliver Twist. When I said aloud, "It is a far, far better thing that I do, than I have ever done . . . " Tears of love filled my eyes at my selflessness.

It is not quite clear where the selflessness lies, but the reader is left with the unambiguous impression that Angelou knows enough about Beowulf to place him in the proper culinary tradition and that she is familiar enough with the work of Charles Dickens to quote him.

Parents' urges to read this and not the other are not uncharacteristic in shaping a child's literacy—but the difference that makes a distinction in the black literary tradition is that parents in the generations of the early to mid-twentieth century often acted in the role of culture-keepers, making certain that knowledge about the race would be both appreciated and passed on. This seems the goal of Angelou's mother's request for James Weldon Johnson. There are many books "about the race" absent from these lists of literary influence, despite their availability to would-be writers and casual readers alike. Du Bois's advice to the Negro father gives just a sampling of this kind of literature. Angela Davis's autobiography includes bookmarks that seem to make an effort to indicate a balance of black and white authors. Noting her "mother's encouragement and prodding" of her reading habit, she also recalls some of the books that she read, and carefully, it seems, balancing the authors she remembers:

a new Black library was built down the hill, on the corner of Center Street and Eighth Avenue . . . with its shiny linoleum floors and varnished tables . . . it became one of my favorite hangouts. For hours at a time, I read avidly there—everything from *Heidi* to Victor Hugo's *Les Misérables,* from Booker T. Washington's *Up from Slavery* to Frank Yerby's lurid novels.[4]

When we wonder over what seem token inclusions of black authors on these lists, there may be a way to understand how or why the weight of this tradition of literature about the race might not be helpful to a writer. James Baldwin takes on this issue directly, suggesting that the tradition and its books add a special burden for consuming a certain kind of information, and for writing from within that informational base, that they actually

> add to the difficulties about being a Negro writer . . . the Negro problem is written about so widely. The bookshelves groan under the weight of information, and everyone therefore considers himself informed. And this information, furthermore, operates usually (generally, popularly) to reinforce traditional attitudes.[5]

Baldwin's parents only urge the Bible onto his reading list—a reflection of their own deep religiosity and at least his father's desire that he become a preacher. Baldwin is ambivalent here, writing at first that his parents' urging turned him away from that text:

> I began plotting novels at about the time I learned to read. . . . In those days my mother was given to the exasperating and mysterious habit of having babies. As they were born, I took them over with one hand and held a book with the other. The children probably suffered, though they have since been kind enough to deny it, and in this way I read *Uncle Tom's Cabin* and *A Tale of Two Cities* over and over and over again; in this way, in fact, I read just about everything I could get my hands on—except the Bible, probably because it was the only book I was encouraged to read.

Just a few pages later, however, when reflecting on what texts and language might have influenced his writing, his response is that

> when one begins looking for influences one finds them by the score. I haven't thought much about my own, not enough anyway; I hazard that the King James Bible, the rhetoric of the store-front church, something ironic and violent and perpetually understated in Negro speech —and something of Dickens' love for bravura—have something to do with me today; but I wouldn't stake my life on it.

One of the reasons we want to know about writers' reading is to guess at their influences, to see if we might be able to detect a certain kind of literary training or the likely effect of another's style. I think writers are (probably necessarily) circumspect when acknowledging this kind of legacy, each wanting to lay claim to the originality and distinction that come from a particular vision shaped by their singular experiences and responses to the world. But writers also invariably respond to the novice's query for the way into their elite company— how might I become a writer?—by advising the questioner to read: widely, deeply, and thoroughly. Baldwin's comment in "Autobiographical Notes" from *Notes of a Native Son* acknowledges a complex set of influences—none particularly from the traditions of the black text, despite the "groan of information" from these available on bookshelves. (I think it interesting that he says here that "the" bookshelves groan—distancing them from possibly being bookshelves of black books in his possession.) We find an additionally culturally inflected text when he makes room for the influence of a black church text— the sermon, which scholars argue has a discrete and insular tradition. Finally, even though Baldwin seems to demur just pages earlier from following his parents' advice to read the Bible, he indicates its likely influence on his own writing.

 తా

The Anchor Bar was a landmark of more than it intended—its renown now widespread in the country and its menu available online.

It marks a waiting place for me that today not only reminds me of the bus ride and the library but feels like a way station on a road toward a certain maturity and independence and toward an appreciation and respect for the preferences my parents expressed. We came, eventually, my parents and I, to share books back and forth with each other: certain ones for Mommy, others for my father—with memories from those moments that, in the times I miss them the most, are deeply satisfying. I recall the time I gave him James Weldon Johnson's autobiography, *Along This Way,* a cloth edition so that it would take its place among the books my father prized. As I recall this, I think I know better the origin of some of my own thinking about which books might be shelved with others. Dad and I enjoyed immensely our discussions about this book, and later, in both our lives, about so many others.

Angelou's effort to please her mother led to her joining the hundreds of thousands of black children who have learned and recited Johnson's "The Creation." My response to my mother's teaching it to me was to look for more like it (eventually committing his "Go Down Death" from *Seven Negro Sermons in Verse* to memory as well), but Angelou merely acknowledges her mother's interest and urging as a bookmark of her mother's value rather than her own, as she continues a story that seems to value love over passion.

One day, when my sister and I came home from school, and John came over with yet another comic book stuffed under his jacket, we hurriedly ran upstairs to place it under our beds. But the box where they had been layered to near overflowing was empty. No sign whatsoever remained of our collection, nor was there any indication of where it had gone, or who removed it. We knew then our comic book days had come to an end. No one ever spoke of them. The next Saturday, when I walked toward the Anchor Bar and then boarded the bus to the library, I chose my books quite carefully, fully aware that there would be no "drivel" to read between library books—but unaware that the moment marked the closing of the distance and a mooring place found between my father's desires and my own.

6

A Proud Chestnut

I've done my reading. All my homework. Should I tell you what I've found? Shall I quote Whitman or Auden or Pound? Shall I give you a Canto or a Quartet? Hughes or Baraka or Hayden? Lincoln or Du Bois? . . . Read to you from my commonplace book, tease you with the profane, the sacred phrases that strike me, struck me? . . . I have them all. Words. . . . They give me no answers.

RANDALL KENAN, *Let the Dead Bury the Dead*

MOM this doesn't make any sense. Ayana had the book open in her hands. It was, as she labeled it, "a chapter book," to distinguish it from the picture books she informed me she had "outgrown." It happened the same moment she no longer wanted baby dolls for gifts but a teenaged Barbie.

I could only sigh. She was a tiny little girl at five, and every once in a while I still had a disconnect between the book in her hand and her size. But her vocabulary and her reading were way past her appearance, so I often had to readjust to acknowledge the distinction between her body and her books. This time, it was a book of fairy tales —I even think it might have been one of the Andrew Lang books— and she had been occupied with them for some time. I took some satisfaction that, at that point, her interests paralleled mine as a youngster (but I wasn't going to be the one to introduce her to comic books), and at that time I had visions of an English major in my head. But she came to me that morning with that puzzled look she could get on her face—frustrated and slightly piqued. She didn't like her reading to be interrupted, and she was used to figuring out the answer herself. I've been trying to figure this out, and the context (yes, she said "context") just doesn't help. I wondered if this was going to be like the other time she had a reading question for me. I was ironing, and I heard her voice shouting out from the recesses of her closet. Mom, what's a period? You know what that is Ayana, a mark you put at the end of a sentence to show that the thought or idea has come to a conclusion. It's in the same class of punctuation as a question mark—indicating the terminal point in a clause; however, if you wanted to join two independent clauses you'd use a . . . — I was about to go into one of my too long explanations, something I did on any occasion I could find, to explain words, roots, meanings, and I'd even do punctuation given the opportunity. This was a narrative she would interrupt as soon as she saw me headed in that direction. No. No she said, no it isn't, it's something that drips. I put down my iron and came directly to the closet. What are you reading?

I was ready to explain all manner of things to her, but this one caught me unawares and unready. Sitting in the closet on her yellow beanbag, she was holding a book by Judy Blume. That explained it. So the day she told me this doesn't make sense and came to me with a book in hand, ready for my explanation, I was anticipating anything. She read the passage to me, "The prince came to the castle on a proud chestnut." I let out a breath. This one I could handle.

Home Schooling

The stories of books and reading that include the interactions black writers have had with their parents offer an intimate glimpse not only into their childhoods but into the ways in which they will represent their early habits of reading. Are the writers singular and self-motivated? Are they directed by well-meaning teachers or patrons? How do they respond to parental intervention, and are these interventions in any way raced—that is, are they moments that parents choose for cultural instruction?

James Weldon Johnson, whose own work eventually became so important to the tradition and the relationship between oratory and reading, writes lovingly in his autobiography, *Along This Way,* about the time spent with his mother in reading and about his mother's creativity. He wrote that she was "artistic . . . a splendid singer," and he recalls that when he was fifteen, "she revealed to me that she had written verse, and showed me a thin sheaf of poems copied out in her almost perfect handwriting." In recalling her to his autobiography, Johnson writes in a way that implies the fragility of the recollections, filling spaces with ellipses as if to indicate that even though these are "intensely vivid" memories, they are vignettes, and that they have for him as much visual memory as they do power of recall. He allows his reader to fill in the spaces:

> I am between five and six years old. . . . In the early evening the lamp in the little parlor is lit. . . . If the weather is chilly, pine logs are sputtering and blazing in the fireplace. . . . I and my brother, who is a tot, are seated on the floor. . . . My mother takes a book and reads. . . . The

book is *David Copperfield.* . . . Night after night I follow the story, always hungry for the next installment. . . . Then the book is *Tales of
a Grandfather.* . . . Then it is a story by Samuel Lover. I laugh till the
tears roll down my cheeks at the mishaps of Handy Andy. And my
brother laughs too, doubtless because he sees me laughing. . . . My
mother's voice is beautiful; I especially enjoy it when she mimics the
Irish brogue and Cockney accents.[1]

The ellipses, which are not mine but his, may represent that Johnson's
memory is halting, but he nevertheless recalls an interesting set of
readings. Dickens appears more than once in the memories of authors
of this tradition and was popular in American homes, especially during the mid-nineteenth century, after American publishing houses re-
printed these books in pirated editions. The popularity of these books
in American households was certainly indebted to this early and, because of the absence of royalties, cheap circulation. Sir Walter Scott's
work was similarly circulated. His histories of Scotland and France
were expressly addressed to his six-year-old grandson, and they forwarded a particular kind of instruction and philosophy of reading.
Scott intended that the language and structure of these books for children and young people would not be attenuated because of their readers' youth but instead would be presented with the same kind of prose
and complexity appropriate for adults. The language of these histories represented his judgment that an artificially simplified language
was inappropriate for the instruction of children. I cannot be certain
that Johnson was aware of Scott's philosophy—he makes no comment regarding the level of reading required here—but he does place
Scott in the familiar company of Dickens, whose prose we recognize
as adult and challenging. Johnson also writes of his mother's mimicry
of dialects and in this way lets his reader know that he is not just list-
ing book titles. Samuel Lover's *Handy Andy: An Irish Tale* would have
afforded his mother great opportunity to imitate dialect and explains
the "Irish brogue" he recalls in his mother's reading.

The works he places in his mother's voice are challenging, interesting, and speak to a certain sophistication of reading and interest. Johnson makes certain the reader of *Along This Way* appreciates that this distinction is his intent by drawing a contrast between his father's interactions with him and his mother's. He writes:

> My father gave me my first own books, a "library" consisting of seven volumes packed in a cardboard case four and a half inches high, three inches wide, and two inches deep. I still have the books; they are intact, but show the passage of the years. Each book contains a story about good little girls and good and bad little boys. I need not add that each story pointed out a wholesome lesson. I list them: *Peter and His Pony,* *The Tent in the Garden, Harry the Shrimper, The White Kitten, Willie Wilson the Newsboy,* and *The Water Melon.*

Johnson then quotes a long portion from *Peter and His Pony,* noting that "the chief effect of the story on me was a long season of importuning my father to buy me a pony—the which [*sic*] I never got."

The attention he accords his father seems a purposeful juxtaposition here to indicate the difference between his mother's and father's judgment of his capabilities. It is his mother's artistic sensibility and background that nurture the development of his aesthetic tastes. His father's underestimation of his reading opens the opportunity for him to note his own reading interests on more than one occasion. Early in his life, in reference to the library of children's books that his father gave him, Johnson writes:

> I finished these little books in short order, and looked for stronger meat. In fact, my father had underestimated my stage of development; my mother's readings had already carried me far beyond books of this grade. I read for myself *Pickwick Papers,* some of *The Waverly Novels, Pilgrim's Progress,* the fairy tales of the Brothers Grimm and took my first dip into poetry through Sir Walter Scott. I think that of these books the stories by the Brothers Grimm made the deepest effect. These stories left me haunted by the elusiveness of beauty—elusiveness, its very

quintessence. Years after, when I read Keats's "Ode to a Nightingale" the thought flashed through my mind that for one whose spirit had not been thus pervaded in childhood it would be impossible even to catch at the tenuous beauty. . . . I exhausted the little supply in our parlor and began laying hands on any book that came within my reach. I remember one day when I was absorbed in a novel I had got hold of with the title, as I remember it, *Vashti—Or Until Death Do Us Part,* my mother said to me, "You had better leave that book till you are older." How good were her grounds for censorship I cannot tell but I remember that I finished the book without, I think, doing myself any appreciable harm.

Vashti was written by the Georgia writer Augusta Jane Wilson in 1869, and like her other novels, it became a best seller. Other than its being a story about women who are disappointed in love, marriage, and career, it is not apparent why Johnson's mother suggested he postpone reading it—except that this was in many ways a woman's novel, within the tradition of domestic fiction, and his mother may have wanted to differentiate his reading from her own. It appears that the books in her parlor may have been the source of his reading. In his allegedly fictional book *Autobiography of an Ex-Colored Man,* Johnson includes a careful description of his mother's library:

I began to explore the glass-doored bookcase. . . . I found there *Pilgrim's Progress,* Peter Parley's *History of the United States,* Grimm's *Household Stories, Tales of a Grandfather,* a bound volume of an old English publication (I think it was called *The Mirror*), a little volume called *Familiar Science,* and somebody's *Natural Theology,* which last, of course, I could not read, but which, nevertheless, I tackled, with the result of gaining a permanent dislike for all kinds of theology. There were several other books of no particular name or merit, such as agents sell to people who know nothing of buying books. How my mother came by this little library which, considering all things, was so well suited to me I never sought to know. . . . At any rate she encouraged in me the habit of reading.

The presence of Scott's *Tales* here, as well as in *Along This Way,* suggests the source is his mother's actual library and makes reasonable some speculation that this list in *Ex-Colored Man* is a more detailed accounting of the books in her parlor collection. It is perhaps a way of filling in the gaps created by the ellipses in his accounting from *Along This Way.* His mother's suggestion that he postpone reading *Vashti* might have been her way of maintaining some distinction between his reading and his presumption that the books within her glass-doored bookcase would be "well-suited" to him. It at least intimated some parental boundaries.

Johnson reads many of the authors that other writers include on their booklists, but he is nearly alone among these writers (until Henry Louis Gates, more than a half a century later) in his frankness about literature that might encourage a fleshly rather than an intellectual response. There are hints of his mother's censorship, or at least of her commentary on and attention to his choices. Further in the autobiography, Johnson takes on a much more contested issue—and it is his father's presence that he selects to form a final commentary on the matter of his reading.

Johnson's language anticipates and is surprisingly parallel to the language of the arguments that would shape the debates surrounding the first amendment and pornography as litigated in *Roth v. United States* in 1957, including commentary that becomes the argument around the notion of community standards and reasonableness. In this section of his autobiography, he recalls a job he held in a surgeon's office, that of a Dr. Summers, during a summer when he was in his late teens and still in preparatory school:

> I explored the books the doctor kept at his office. The number was not large but the range was wide. . . . A corner of the doctor's shelves was devoted to *erotica;* there I found the *Decameron* of Boccaccio and the *Droll Stories* of Balzac. It would be interesting, at least to me, if I could now determine what effect on me these forbidden books had. I can somewhat recall the low that pervaded my body and my mind as I read some of these stories. Others of the stories struck me as very

funny. I was stirred and entertained; was I damaged? The whole case for censorship is in that question. I cannot see that these books had the slightest deleterious effect. And I do not believe that any normal person is in any manner damaged by such reading. I grant that on persons of abnormal instincts or weaknesses there may not be this lack of bad effects, but those persons are anyhow bound to get at certain facts about life, and probably form sources far more contaminating than the wit and delicacy of Boccaccio and Balzac and the other masters of erotic literature. Did these books do me any good? That is a question the advocates of censorship might follow up with, but it raises a point not involved.

Johnson's 1933 reflection on this period was deeply introspective. It had already formed the basis of an important story line in his novel *Autobiography of an Ex-Colored Man,* and a careful reader might reasonably come to understand the relationship between Johnson and Summers as one prompted by the older man's intimate interest in his young apprentice. Johnson certainly sees Dr. Summers as a representation of a certain version of cosmopolitanism that he coveted and later modeled. By the time he writes the autobiography, he had already lived in close association with the bohemian world of New York artists—prompted in part by his brother Rosamund's musical career. Would this contact with a more liberal and less rigid world of the arts encourage him in this autobiographical moment?

Johnson's relationship with Summers leaves sufficient room in *Along This Way* for speculation that the older man's interest was not entirely paternal, and this possibility is more fully intimated in the semi-autobiographical *Ex-Colored Man.* There he writes of a "familiar and warm relationship" with his mentor and explains how his "patron" "had a decided personal liking for me."[2] He wrote that "between this peculiar man and me there had grown a very strong bond of affection" and that finally, when he decided to break off the relationship his patron offered, the elder man's farewell was accomplished "almost coldly," leaving the ex-colored character/Johnson to wonder "whether he was in a hurry to get rid of what he considered a fool, or whether he was striving to hide deeper feelings."

In one sense it is unfair to read the autobiography and the novel against each other, but there is sufficient parallelism to much of Johnson's actual history to understand why the novel's anonymous publication in 1912 was met with speculation that it was not entirely a fiction. In *Along This Way,* Johnson and the doctor traveled together to New York and Washington during that summer, sleeping in the same hotel room, "a double room in which both of us slept," and the doctor had "formed a strong affection for me which he did not hide." For Johnson's part, he admired the doctor's worldliness. To eliminate that one summer's experience from his autobiography would have occasioned a censorship that did not honor his mentor for the model he clearly represented to the teenager. The occasion of this relationship gained further pathos and significance in young Johnson's life when he learned that sometime after they parted, his mentor committed suicide—an occasion left open for speculation that the elder man's loss of the younger was not unreasonably attached to the event.

To erase the impact or presence of the library in the doctor's office would have been, in effect, to erase the doctor's importance in his development. In an age when black male writers struggled mightily against the stereotypes of hypersexuality attached to black men and went to extremes to qualify and note their intellectualism, Johnson uncharacteristically breaks that mold with this frank engagement with a literature that acknowledges a "forbidden" text. This reading may explain as well the next passage, in which he marks a certain book as earning his father's antipathy:

> From the doctor's library I read some of Montaigne's essays, Thomas Paine's *Age of Reason,* and Robert Ingersoll's *Some Mistakes of Moses* and *The Gods and Other Lectures.* I was so much impressed with *The Age of Reason* that I carried it along with me so that I could read and reread it. One day my father summarily commanded me to "take that book out of the house and never bring it here again." I don't believe he was

familiar with the book. Whether this stern action was prompted by having scanned it at the time or by "Tom" Paine's popular reputation, I do not know. Indeed, I was too much astounded by the sudden show of intolerance on my father's part to question the reason.

One way a reader might understand what seems to be his father's overreaction to a book he was not familiar with is to wonder whether at this point it may not have been the particular book itself but perhaps his father's growing wariness and mistrust, or perhaps jealousy of the strong relationship forming between Dr. Summers and his son —and the way in which his son's bond with that book from Summers suggested an intimacy the father wished to avoid, or saw as competition for his own stature in his still young son's life. Even though there need not have been any reciprocated desire on young Johnson's part, the book and his attachment to it may have come to symbolize a relationship that provoked his father's disapproval.

Culture Keepers

Parents' urging and censorship, but mostly their attention to their children's reading habits, form a significant dimension of the way in which these writers recall reading—whether it is a deeply complicated memory like Johnson's, or the kind of memory that simply passes on parents' values, rituals, or interest in their children's learning something about the race.

When poet Nikki Giovanni recounts that her mother asked her to read three books, "one of which was *Black Boy*," it is possible to see the cycle of readers and writers coming into a shared racial space as they were introduced to the literature of the culture's traditions. Giovanni recalls that she took the book her mother recommended to school in the seventh grade "and the nun called it trash. Which was beautiful," Giovanni reflects, "because I could intellectually isolate all white nuns as being dumb and unworthy of my attention."[3] But rather than exploring her defensive response to the nun who had essentially censored and disparaged a book that her mother had selected, Giovanni uses the occasion to reflect on an association between reading and parenting that helps put into perspective the exchanges that happen between parent and child over books, and the ways in which those moments extend themselves beyond the occasion. It is an occasion that illustrates the contest that often occurred between the black parent and the school in terms of the cultural messages that African American parents might pass on to their children, and the contradiction of the value they would assign to culture that schooling could represent. But children read both of these assignments, understand the conflict between parents and schools, or the reinforcement, and still manage to develop their own agendas. Giovanni does not write further about that encounter but uses the autobiographical moment about her reading to explain that she was "really turned on to Greek and Roman mythology—the gods and goddesses towering over everybody in their exclusive god club. And I would think if ever I was a goddess I would take it all seriously, and not eat pomegranates or fall in love with anyone other than a god and I would bear proud sons and train them correctly."

There's much in these relationships among books and parents and reading in the African American tradition that suggests the training is not only about growing up, but growing up properly informed about race. And it is within that qualifier that the racialized difference comes to matter. Giovanni's mother did not casually add *Black Boy* to the three books her daughter was to read. Giovanni was in seventh grade and obviously in a school where racialized pronouncements were likely to be made by people with some authority. Her mother's advice here was, I suspect, a direct intervention in that likelihood, and Giovanni's note about training sons "correctly" might be read into a similar context of caution and care.

I thought I had a young literati in the making, with Ayana's early reading and imaginative writing. But while in elementary school she announced that would become an astrophysicist. She later admitted that she chose astrophysicist because she liked the sound of the word.

7

The Children's Room

To fling my arms wide
In some place of the sun,
To whirl and to dance
Till the white day is done.
. . . .
That is my dream!

LANGSTON HUGHES, "Dream Variation"

I LEARNED to love reading in a castle of a room in a county library. The bookshelves in the children's room were, from my romantic perspective, quite appropriately shelved in a turret. A window seat that followed this curved cloister within the library's tower was my nesting space, and shelved just beneath that seat were the fairy tales, myths, and legends. I discovered them one day when I was looking for a book tucked away beneath the level of my eyesight. I don't recall which books accompanied me to that nest before I looked to the shelves below. But I do remember the breathlessness when I discovered the tales of Andrew Lang: the books that were titled with their rainbow hues—red, purple, blue, green—a full series of magic that promised complete escape wrapped round the arc of that enchanting space.

Miss Silk was the librarian in the children's room. She was nearly as translucent as her name—a wisp of a woman, quiet, elderly, and encouraging of my bookish silences. She interfered only to lead me to other places in that library to gather books, and then she would bring us both back to that nook in the children's room. Andrew Lang's fairy tales fell quickly to other fiction. To my father's distress and disapprobation, I was not much interested then in nonfiction. I wanted those library shelves to give me only those worlds imagined. I do recall reading and being fascinated with travel narratives—the voyage of the *Kon-Tiki,* Magellan's Pacific sojourn to Easter Island and the perils of that turbulent strait—those tales of adventure were like a fiction in my world. But what was most important was that I felt no boundaries in that library—there was room for me in its expanse. There were no shelves I could not claim, no books beyond my reach. If they were, Miss Silk would bring them down to me, or over to me, or walk me back to the children's room from those older readers' spaces, back to where, I think now, both of us found sanctuary. My county library was built as I needed it to be—a magical space with massive bricks and winding stairways. Its turrets and heft seemed right and appropriate. And although I remember it fully as a splendid and welcoming space, mine is a memory now mediated by my adult understanding of that library system's perspective on "Negro" librarians. I suspect as well that Miss Silk was indeed among those extraordinary human beings of the time who made certain that the prejudices that surrounded these institutions would not injure a child, like me, who was marked as a reader.

Politics and Prose

Recalling these places and the way in which our memories of books are shaped by their surround seems a mark of writers in this tradition. In *The Big Sea,* the first of Langston Hughes's two autobiographies, he writes:

> In Topeka, as a small child, my mother took me with her to the little vine-covered library on the grounds of the Capitol. There I first fell in love with librarians, and I have been in love with them ever since— those very nice women who help you find wonderful books! The silence inside the library, the big chairs, and long tables, and the fact that the library was always there and didn't seem to have a mortgage on it, or any sort of insecurity about it—all of that made me love it. And right then, even before I was six, books began to happen to me, so that after a while, there came a time when I believed in books more than in people—which, of course, was wrong.[1]

Hughes writes of a library's security and dependability, seemingly in distinction to the kinds of worries a child might have whose moving and homeplaces had troublesome attachments to a family's finances. It was less important for him to remark about the books that mattered to him, but his readers still get a visceral sense of the comfort he found in that library. He does not, however, leave books out of those spaces of his remembrance, writing that "the only poems I liked as a child were Paul Laurence Dunbar's. And *Hiawatha*. But I liked any kind of stories. I read all of my mother's novels from the library: *The*

Buffalo Public Library, ca. 1890. Photo courtesy of the Buffalo and Erie County Historical Society.

Topeka Library, Kansas. Photo courtesy of the Kansas State Historical Society.

Rosary, The Mistress of Shenstone, Freckles, Edna Ferber, all of Harold
Bell Wright, and all of Zane Grey. I thought *Riders of the Purple Sage* a
wonderful book and still think so, as I remember it."

Hughes's childhood reading is unmarked by the kind of specific
commentary that noted he was reading black authors. In this regard,
his mention is unlike that of some of the other writers of the tradition,
whose commentary might include a "the only" or some other comment that would mark their reading as racialized. Hughes is careful, however, to mark the kind of literary heritage that he wants the
reader to associate with his artistic sensibility. He writes about how,
when he was in high school in Cleveland, Ohio, he would read himself to sleep with a passage that echoes Du Bois in its bathos, and in its
implicit appeal to the reader to consider its author as not only someone for whom a classic literature is appealing but as someone who
finds an intimacy within that tradition unlike any other.

> Reading Schopenhauer and Nietzsche, and Edna Ferber and Dreiser,
> and de Maupassant in French. I never will forget the thrill of first un-
> derstanding the French of de Maupassant. The soft snow was falling
> through one of his stories in the little book we used in school, and that
> I had worked over so long, before I really felt the snow falling there.
> Then all of a sudden one night the beauty and the meaning of the
> words in which he made the snow fall, came to me. I think it was de
> Maupassant who made me really want to be a writer and write stories
> about Negroes, so true that people in far-away lands would read them
> —even after I was dead.

The difference between Du Bois and Hughes is, of course, the last sentence of this literary confessional, where Hughes remarks that it was
this kind of association between text and language that compelled
him to write about Negroes, with the hope that his work would re-
verberate with the same truths that he found in de Maupassant. The
similarity is that both Hughes and Du Bois manage to establish and
to claim a literary lineage and inspiration that links them to the traditions most respected in the era of their writing.

Nikki Giovanni seems to share a similar interest in making apparent her interests in the classics—but the critical difference for Giovanni, a poet who came of age during the Black Arts era, is that she credits Gwendolyn Brooks's work with being the first to stir her interest in poetry. In *Gemini,* Giovanni, like other artists of the century, makes a point of emphasizing the importance of her reading, interspersing her habits of reading among other comments about her emerging aesthetic: "I would slyly hint from behind one of those history books I used to be hung up with that it's best to do what is best for you and then you never have to expect something back. . . . I was always just a little secreted away with the thought that one day I would be understood. This is probably a main reason any artist emerges."

Giovanni lets her readers know, even though it seems hidden in another point, that she was an inveterate reader of history. In a rhetorically strategic move that shadows the tradition of Du Bois and Hughes yet reflects the intense Black Arts aesthetic of the age as she claims her relationship to Gwendolyn Brooks and "black books," Giovanni manages to let her reader know that there are poets outside of the black tradition who have made an intellectual difference in her development. The paragraph begins with what seems both a suggestion to her readers as well as an intimation about herself: "I've been slow to make evaluations. My life style was that I read about fifty books a year and absorbed them and then related them to another level. And I tried to read Black books. I remember reading 'Annie Allen' and being pleased for the first time with poetry. But I didn't pursue it. I went on to Pound and Eliot because it filled an empty spot in my head."[2] It is not clear here what Giovanni did not pursue. Was it reading black books? Reading poetry? It doesn't seem to be the latter, because in the next sentence she explains that what substance she needed to "fill the empty spot" came from Ezra Pound and T. S. Eliot.

Writing betwixt and between these traditions reflects both the skill of authorship as well as the fact of living in that same medial space—where access, acclamation, or approbation often made the difference in choosing what one read, or what one reported as read.

Langston Hughes's portrait of himself as an adult artist begins with the opening scene of his autobiography—making apparent the relationship of books to his maturity as well as to his independence:

> Melodramatic maybe. . . . But then it was like throwing a million bricks out of my heart when I threw the books into the water. I leaned over the rail of the S.S. *Malone* and threw the books as far as I could out into the sea—all the books I had had at Columbia, and all the books I had lately bought to read. The books went down into the moving water in the dark off Sandy Hook. Then I straightened up, turned my face to the wind, and took a deep breath. . . . I felt grown, a man, inside and out.

When he chooses a different corpus, he turns to the ship's library, perhaps a symbolic accounting for the way in which his reading was unmoored from the constraints of a university's curriculum and was interpretively closer to the metaphor that inaugurated his vocation. Hughes writes evocatively of "those long winter nights with snow swirling down the Hudson, and the old ships rocking and creaking in the wind, and the ice scraping and crunching against their sides, and the steam hissing in the radiators were ideal for reading. I read all the ship's library. I found there Butler's *The Way of All Flesh,* Conrad's *Heart of Darkness,* and d'Annunzio's *The Flame of Life.*"

The books Hughes chooses to remember specifically here seem intensely thoughtful and deliberate. Here, I suspect, it is less important that the reader know the substance of these books. Instead, these are books whose provocative and deeply imagistic titles—flesh, heart, darkness, flame, and life—collected in this way, formulate an intimation, or at least a suggestion, of the passions that a reader might as a consequence of this list associate with Hughes. Is this an intentional set of books? The form of autobiography as a selective and organized narrative would suggest that it is.

The associations between book and body are differently enacted for writers of the twentieth century. Some seem to have worked more cautiously over the representations of what would make them an unimpeachable source on matters having to do with race. This effort seems especially pronounced among those for whom their public recognition depended on their continued presence on a literary scene, or even on their presence as public spokespersons. In contrast to the lists of these literary figures, bookmarks by someone for whom the autobiography was a mere record of a life lived in activist engagement with the civil rights politics of race and gender in the twentieth century appear to be more coincidental than strategic.

Pauli Murray, the first black woman to become an Episcopal priest, was also a feminist, civil rights lawyer, and one of the founding members of the National Organization for Women. The focus of her life was her activism in women's equity and civil rights, and in making plain the disjunction in each movement: in women's rights, for the concerns of black people; and in civil rights, for the status of women. When she became an Episcopal priest, she used the pulpit to continue a call to be "poet, lawyer, teacher and friend," finally finding the "spirit of love and reconciliation" as expressed in her ministry as the "goal of human wholeness."[3] Murray's focus never seemed to be directed toward sculpting a public recognition of her own gifts and talents but was rather outwardly directed toward explaining how her specific background led to the activism that would characterize her adult life. In her autobiography, published posthumously by her estate, she describes her reading in ways that echo those who have written of reading within the intimacy and safety of their family homes. Her list sounds as indiscriminate as she represents it to be:

> I spent long hours in [my aunt's] parlor working my way through the small collection of books in the bookcase. I read indiscriminately, devouring the contents of such incongruous volumes as *Dying Testimonies of the Saved and Unsaved; Stoddard's Lectures; Works of Paul Laurence Dunbar; Chambers's Encyclopedia; The Remarkable Advancement of the Afro-American Negro from the Bondage of Slavery, Ignorance and Poverty to the Freedom of Citizenship, Intelligence, Affluence, Honor and Trust*, published in 1899; and Booker T. Washington's *Up From Slavery.*

This list includes the pamphlet published in 1902 by John Gibson, *The Remarkable Advancement,* which contains a series of photographic images of African Americans from earliest days of picking cotton to the later portraits of model citizens such as "a prominent leader in Chicago" and a "Leading Club Woman and High School Teacher, Kansas City." Some of these women may have served as visual images of what the young Murray might aspire to. The touching and lugubrious testimonials in Solomon Shaw's 1898 *Dying Testimonies,* from "Ma, I Can't Die until You Promise Me" to "I Hear the Angels Singing around My Bed" or "I Am as Much Lost as Though I Were in Hell," would make as absorbing reading today as they must have for the young Murray in the early 1900s. Another book of images was John Stoddard's *Lectures,* a photographic collection of travel talks—from Lake Como to India to the American West—that would easily have absorbed a young reader's imagination. There are no books here that seem selected to tell us anything more than what might have been available in her aunt's parlor. Underscoring this straightforwardness, she even writes about what she did not read, despite its availability on her aunt's shelves. The confession does not add to a case of deep intellectualism and curiosity, but it continues to contribute to the story that Murray weaves when she writes that "Aunt Pauline also had a set of English literary works and a ten-volume series on American history, which included four novels based on the major wars the United States had then fought. I skipped the history text and read the novels many times. I also read the few novels I found by Gene Stratton Porter, Ellen Glasgow, and Zane Grey."

Murray takes important note of the presence of those same magazines that Du Bois was to suggest as essential to the "Negro Father," making it just a bit more curious that other writers in this tradition either did not have the magazines in their home or failed to mark them as important. Murray writes: "I grew up with copies of *The Crisis* in our home, the NAACP publication which I knew had produced its first issue in the year and month of my birth [1910]." But it is her record of the library and her childhood reading that makes her entire accounting seem like a record rather than a testimony:

When I had exhausted our slender supply of books, I began to make trips to the Durham Colored Library, a small one-room collection in a

Children leaving Stanford L. Warren Library, Durham, North Carolina. Photo courtesy of the Durham County Library, Durham, North Carolina.

building at the corner of Fayetteville and Pettigrew streets near the Southern Railroad tracks. Mrs. Wooton, the librarian, steered me toward the children's books and I gobbled up *The Bobbsey Twins, The Five Little Peppers and How They Grew, The Boy Allies* series, and the nature-story books *Frank the Young Naturalist, Frank in the Woods,* and *Frank on the Prairie.* One year I won first prize among the colored children for having read the most books in the library. The prize, a fountain pen, was presented to me by General Julian S. Carr, a man my folks called "a true Southern aristocrat." The presentation ceremony and General Carr's words of praise made me feel very proud of my achievement.

Murray's record here marks her childhood, its achievements, her sustained habits of reading, and the ways in which the habit may be understood to have contributed to her later vocation. By noting the volume *Dying Testimonies,* she suggests her potential life in the ministry. But it is the habit, not the list, that she chooses to make known to her readers—a distinction, it seems, from other writers in this tradition. Like these writers, Murray also recalls the spaces where this reading occurred and the way in which those spaces formed her association with an especially nurtured childhood.

Even though this seems only a story about race and identity, it is important to understand that these spaces did not protect a child from those instincts that had nothing to do with race. For some, like science fiction writer Octavia Butler, the very idea of a designated children's room was enough to keep her out of the library. Butler recalls that in her Pasadena, California, library she "was restricted to a section of the library called the 'Peter Pan Room.' That had the effect of stopping me from going to the library much, because after a while I felt insulted by the juvenile books." Butler did not return to the library until she was fourteen and had "graduated" to the adult section.

ت

I have later come to wonder at the ease of those early years—the ways in which the library was, for me, a space that was free from anything but the wonder of those books. This is a luxury of memory absolutely mediated by the knowledge that I was fortunate in a way other children of my color were not, and that I was fortunate in having the hand of Miss Silk to lend me the whole of the library, and still to find a reading space I cherished in the tower seat of the children's room. When I look at the images of the Buffalo Library and the Memphis Library, which look so much alike, it is plain that despite their similarity, what was a shelter for me was a fortress for Richard Wright. Beneath the image, matters of race and culture, family and self mediate the experiences of our lives. Even the deliberate designation of a "public" space may indeed have private consequences that linger.

My reading in the children's room—full, open, and unrestricted—contributed mightily to the ways I read the world today—still wanting the fictive sanctuary of another's imagination, sensing that my adult pleasure in science fiction came first from those variously hued fairy books, the brothers Grimm, and Hans Christian Andersen. Whether or not books are routes toward something other than their own imaginary seems to depend on the writer's need to use them to make a point far removed from the *sometimes* sanctuary of the children's room.

8

My Mother's Singing

You will need a song . . . take some Billie Holiday for the sad days and some Charlie Parker for the happy ones but always keep at least one good Spiritual for comfort.

NIKKI GIOVANNI, *Quilting the Black-Eyed Pea*

M
Y mother was singing even when she did not realize it. She sang through washing and ironing, sang when driving or riding, sang, she told us, when visiting the Holy Land and atop the Mount of Olives. She sent us a postcard letting us know that, when she ascended the mount and looked out at the city, she sang spirituals—"Twelve Gates to the City" and "Jerusalem." On other occasions mother would sing hymns or anthems, songs from the Unitarian church choir or from Bethel A.M.E.'s hymnals. My favorite was, and still is, "Great Is Thy Faithfulness." She did not need a choir to sing, or an audience; it was probably the only mindless activity she ever did. It was natural, instinctive, and a gift of spirit.

If there was a choir, however, mother was a member. One of the moments when I felt I understood her best was when, twenty-five years after she had graduated from Talladega, I joined its choir. I had the benefit of the last magical years of the legendary Dr. Frank Harrison—who educated and directed that choir in musical traditions from around the world and who insisted that we would never, ever sing a spiritual with accompaniment. We sang them a cappella, as they were traditionally sung in the African American tradition, and they were never more beautifully rendered. I was in the last class of Talladegans to benefit from Dr. Harrison's rigor and dedication. He had been there when both mother and father were enrolled, and so we came to share the legacy of training and appreciation for music learned under his tutelage. When I came home from college, Mother, Daddy, and I could sing together "In Bright Mansions" or "Behold That Star!" I recognize and deeply treasure the legacy of Talladega that I could share with my parents, and that I share today with my husband. I think it not accidental that I met my husband, Russell, in the college choir, and that our many years of marriage have something to do with the foundation of the way in which we learned, under Dr. Harrison, how music and spirit, culture and character, might be built and sustained.

After mother retired from the Buffalo public school system, and when it came time for a church program, she rescued an old text of *Heaven Bound,* an African American folk drama that follows a group of pilgrims—sinners and saints both—hoping to make heaven their home. Characters such as The Wayward Girl, Saint Peter, Satan, and The Striver make up the cast. Pilgrims try to avoid Satan's temptation as they sing a spiritual or hymn from the African American tradition —walking down the aisles of the church trying mightily to reach the heavenly gates while Satan follows with taunts and bribes. The congregation is caught in the drama of who will succumb or who might actually reach heaven's gates, placing Satan "behind" him. It was a high drama and an artistry made for my mother's talents. When she taught seventh- and eighth-grade language arts, the highlight of the school year at Genesee Humboldt Junior High was her annual production of either Sophocles' *Antigone* or Thornton Wilder's *Our Town.* How I wished I could have been in her classes and been assigned the role of Antigone or Emily. I knew their roles by heart. I spent many an hour after school sitting in the auditorium during rehearsals, repeating after the specially selected Emily who gets to say, "It goes so fast, we don't have time to look at it." My mother lavished attention on these productions, and her creativity in staging and imagination and her inspiration to twelve- and thirteen-year-old actors are legendary. These were the assigned dramas that met the curriculum, but Mother outdid any teacher's guide. After she retired and was left to her own devices, she was untethered from the curricular requirements, and so it was the 1940s African American church mystery play *Heaven Bound* that earned her talents for drama, song, and production, satisfied her cultural sensibility, and led to her being publicly acknowledged as a culture-keeper.

The Textures of Tradition

There is a close association between song and text in African America, and I suspect it has something to do with the frequency with which writers of this tradition make mention of both music and books in the same passage—seeing one as a complement, or at least a dimension, of the other. John Hope Franklin, like James Weldon Johnson, associates his mother with his introduction to these traditions. Franklin writes seamlessly of books and music. After the passage that recounts his mother's teaching about "Negro authors," he notes that she

> also told us about some of the world's great music such as Handel's Oratorio "Esther," in which she had sung in college. While the music at school was interesting and lively, especially after I achieved the position of first trumpet in the band and orchestra, there was no Handel or Mozart, or Beethoven. We had a full fare of Victor Herbert and John Philip Sousa, and operettas, in more than one of which I sang the leading role.[1]

After writing of the books he read in his mother's parlor, James Weldon Johnson connects the moment to his musical training, writing, in the very next paragraph, that "my mother was also my first music teacher. She had less than ordinary proficiency on the organ and piano, but she knew enough to give me and my brother a start."[2] Johnson's *Autobiography of an Ex-Colored Man* elaborates on the description of his mother's attentive instruction, but here the main character is a pianist rather than writer.

It is, however, C. Eric Lincoln's booklist that may well be the measure of all others of the tradition, both in the hubris it expresses and in its choice of representation. His is actually a catalog of authors and also composers. Like Franklin's and Johnson's, Lincoln's mention of music is accomplished within the same moment that the autobiography attends to a description of books that mattered.

Lincoln was a widely acclaimed and prolific scholar of religion and culture, the author of over twenty volumes of scholarship, a novel, and a collection of poetry. *Coming Through the Fire: Surviving Race and Place in America* distills fifty years of journals and notebooks he had kept, documenting his meditations on race and culture. Although these "Notes on Race" were destroyed in a fire, the work is presented as autobiographical reflections. The book begins with stories from his childhood, and it spends some time explaining to the reader how to understand the distinctiveness of his schooling. He opens this discussion by separating out his education from that of other black youth in Athens, Alabama. Lincoln attended a private school, not unlike several available in the South to black youth at the time (including Palmer Memorial Institute in North Carolina and Pineywoods in Mississippi). But his description of Trinity leaves the reader with the impression that it was the only one of its kind. He also labors over a distinction that is clearly important to him—the privileged bias associated with things northern rather than southern. Lincoln makes certain we understand that his school's staff, and even its supplies, originated in the North.

> At Trinity School, I was safely in the hands of the "outsiders" from Boston, New London, New Haven, and other citadels of Yankee determination, while my friends and counterparts "out in the country" were treated by the state of Alabama to five to seven months of "schooling" each year in one-room shacks. . . . But at Trinity I was fortunate enough to receive the best education available in the area provided by dedicated New England spinsters.[3]

Locating his teachers' backgrounds echoes a distinction that was also important to Malcolm X—who would later become his close friend and colleague. Malcolm X's autobiography recalled how his classes in the Norfolk Prison Colony library were taught by "instructors who came from such places as Harvard and Boston universities." In matters of culture, the South was frequently disparaged. This fact, joined with the South's history of vigorous segregation, seemed to make it especially important to writers who were educated in the South to separate themselves from this geography. In his volume, Lincoln has already established some of the framework of what he considers his elite lineage. So when it comes to the moment of his booklist, he uses it to document the privilege he has assumed as well as the bias that he subtly but assiduously continues, as he makes apparent that he had access to privileges associated with the North rather than the South:

> At Trinity I read everything the library could afford and everything my delighted Yankee schoolmarms could import for me—Walter Scott, Dryden, Pope, Goethe, Ovid, Pushkin, Plutarch, Milton, Plato, Aesop, Washington Irving, and the Transcendentalists. I also read the entire Bible at least three times. And in one of the barrels of clothing, books, and other reusables sent down from the North to be distributed at the school, I found the works of Karl Marx, Lenin, and Adam Smith, and read them inter alia with H. G. Wells, Kafka, Victor Hugo, Dostoyevski, Tolstoy, John Dewey, Richard Wright and all the poets of the Harlem Renaissance.

That Wright and "all the poets" of the Harlem Renaissance are found at the end of this vaunted list might seem an unremarkable incident of placement. "All the poets" could be just a useful generalization of text. But the generalization stands in stark contrast to the detail of the list that precedes it and, by comparison, raises a question of why the other authors were specifically named but not these. Instead, they are placed in a clause that both joins them to Richard Wright and distinguishes them from the rest of the list. There is no other way to read this but to understand that these black authors are an afterthought. It is also worth noting that Lincoln does not give the titles of books—only authors. This is a choice that, in comparison with other authors' lists in this tradition, seems a distinction with a difference. A booklist that includes titles seems a more intimate and even more genuine remembrance. Annotating authors only, especially in such numbers as appear here, is distant, and distancing. But it is also consistent, because Lincoln follows this catalog with a similarly impressive list of composers. Once again, at its end, we find an anomaly. This time it is not a group of composers but a group of performers. And here too are the black folk that seem, at least in this formulation, an afterthought:

twice a week (and any other time I could cadge the key to the school music room) I sat enraptured in another world listening to the music that poured out of the wind-up Victrola that stood gleaming majestically in mahogany and brass, waiting to share the wondrous works of Wagner, Beethoven, Schubert, Verdi, Bach, Strauss, Brahms, Rachmaninoff and the Fisk Jubilee Singers.

The Jubilee Singers, the world-renowned black group from Fisk University, whose travels and concerts once earned the school its endowment, are critically important to the musical legacy of the era as well as to the traditions of African American culture in both the nineteenth and twentieth centuries. But the fact that they, along with Wright and the Harlem Renaissance poets, appear in the last spaces suggests that Lincoln's point was to make it overwhelmingly apparent to his reader that the balance of his education weighs in with the best of the classical, Euro-American traditions. It reinforces his point that his pedigree was unlike the others of his community. As if to underscore exactly that circumstance, Lincoln writes:

> Certainly my opportunities were not typical, for none of those would have been remotely possible in any school or academic program the South provided for its black children. But thinking was going on among black people at whatever levels of opportunity and experience circumstances happened to permit, that thinking was destined to become a countermind to the mind Cash recognized as the only significant expression of the southern perception of reality—past, present, and to come.

Lincoln writes here against the argument of W. G. Cash's 1941 publication, *The Mind of the South,* heralded for its "penetrating and persuasive" analysis of the American South, a "'*white* mind' in Cash's terms, a 'superior mind' of the 'best people.'" One way to understand the lengthy itemization of authors and composers that Lincoln includes in this memoir is that they serve as evidence against the point

Cash articulated in this very popular book. His outrage at this thin analysis takes the form of a documentation of a "mind" that did not match the Cash stereotype. In other words, his illustration of how different in degree and distinction were the quality and training of his own mind may have been a strategy to discount the impact of Cash's critique. His own intellectual pedigree was certainly sufficient contradiction for the "blunderous misperception" in Cash's book; further, it borrows for support the bias of a superiority of all things northern—books delivered in boxes from the North, as well as teachers. Nevertheless, there is a distinct and disappointing hubris in Lincoln's list, and its hierarchy is tediously impressed upon his reader, even though we come to understand and perhaps even appreciate his motivation in making these self-conscious claims, given the pages that precede it regarding the persuasive text of W. G. Cash.

The Fisk Jubilee Singers still sing today—recalling the concerts and performances of their first years as a choral group in 1871, making certain that the legacy of the university and its music survive. Lincoln's recollection of them marks the highest accomplishments of literature and music and is absolutely appropriate, if not just a bit suspect in its singularity. Nevertheless, it makes apparent an intimacy between black text and black music not often acknowledged. Ralph Ellison knows that relationship. His notation regarding books leads to a longer commentary on the oral traditions that are important to the black text. His roll call of books recalls C. Eric Lincoln's mention of New England educators:

> I read my first Shaw and Maupassant, my first Harvard Classics in the home of a friend whose parents were products of that stream of New England education which had been brought to Negroes by the young and enthusiastic white teachers who staffed the schools set up for the freedmen after the Civil War. These parents were both teachers and there were others like them in our town.[4]

But Ellison uses this mention as a transition to a commentary about the complex oral tradition informing his writing, recalling contemporary writer James Baldwin's comment that he was particularly attentive to "the rhetoric of the store-front church, something ironic and violent and perpetually understated in Negro speech." Ellison writes more expansively than Baldwin about

> the places where a rich oral literature was truly functional were the churches, the schoolyards, the barbershops, the cotton-picking camps; places where folklore and gossip thrived. . . . long before I thought of writing, I was claimed by weather, by speech rhythms, by Negro voices and their different idioms, by husky male voices and by the high shrill singing voices of certain Negro women, by music.

Joining this chorus of black writers influenced by oral traditions is novelist Leon Forrest, whose essay "At Home in the Windy City" mentions briefly that Shakespeare's *Othello,* Faulkner, and Tennessee Williams were important to his work; his sustained commentary, however, is on the oral tradition. Forrest writes:

> As a writer who comes out of a culture steeped in the eloquence of the Oral Tradition, I've come to see the Negro preacher as the Bard of the race; and throughout my novels, that rich lodestone of eloquence has provided me with an important springboard. . . . I had been listening to sermons all of my life; but at the time, I was overwhelmed by so many art forms of performance and celebration in the black community, and had little confidence in my abilities to make something magical of the overpowering voices I heard all about me.[5]

He comes to understand the association between the community and neighborhood voices around him, earlier authors in the black tradition, and the idea of the sermon itself as a textual form having an extraordinary potential as literary source. And it is within this discussion that we learn of writers he has read, and what sense he has made of this reading:

> James Weldon Johnson's *God's Trombones;* Faulkner's Negro preacher, Reverend Shegog (named for a Southern white general); Ellison's uses

of the form both in his magnificent novel and works in progress; the sermons in Joyce's *Portrait of the Artist as a Young Man;* John Donne's sermons; and Reverend Mapple's sermon in *Moby Dick,* finally got me energized into the possibility of seeing my way into the texture of the sermon as a seminal source, not only to my culture, but into my own fledgling art. And as the very source for reinvention and transformation of the self, in character.

ﻩ❧

There's a thread between music and text in African America that reverberates like no other tradition. So the ways in which I remember my mother's singing, and her writing, directing, and teaching, and the fact that my husband tells me today that he suspects I write with a primary consciousness of how words sound are related to this complex weave in our culture's texts. One Christmas, my sisters and I each received the same book from my mother, *Songs of Zion,* a songbook from the African American church tradition that was developed for the United Methodist Church—the denomination of mother's later years. Inside the front cover she wrote, "for my children, so that they might remember. Love, Mother."

I do remember. I remember her singing and I remember seeing her in the choir loft of her last church, Lincoln Memorial. We'd sit in the pew with Dad, and I'm certain now that his whole reason for being there was so that he might look up and see his beloved Ouida. When she was weary and her body challenged from the illness that finally took her life, she still made it to church just so she could sing. My mother's singing added days and depth to those last years.

I did not need the *Songs of Zion* to assure these memories. I still hear her voice in my heart every day, but sometimes it is my own song that emerges and I hear my daughter saying, you're singing Mom, and I will look at her surprised that what I thought was merely a lyric in my head was heard. *Songs of Zion* is in an old leather book cover that was a gift from someone I cherished. The new hymnal, slipped into a cover whose worn leather tracery betrays its age, sits atop the old upright piano that is against the wall in our library. It is a reasonable room for both of them. On the piano is a small photograph of my mother, sitting at a piano in her home, practicing the choir's Sunday hymns.

Book. Text. Voice. Memory. Song. Book. They are all within the circle embraced in my mother's singing.

9

Reading Race

I hope instead to sketch, as honestly and as effectively as I can, something I can recognize as my own, aware that as I do so that even as I work after honesty and accuracy, memory will make this only one possible fiction among the myriad—many in open conflict.

SAMUEL R. DELANY, *The Motion of Light in Water*

I READ a certain kind of book while traveling. I call them airport novels. I have bought certain books in airports that have surprised me, but many of them I purchase because I know it will be the kind of novel that I can leave for the next reader in the pocket of the airplane on the return trip home. They usually don't make it to my home library. I read them quickly and, admittedly, sometimes carelessly. And sometimes my interests shape what I am reading into something different from the actual text. So when I read John Grisham's *The Firm,* the fragment of a sentence I read that became definitive said, "the firm had never hired a black"—and I was off in my imaginary. Completely disregarding the clause before, and reading the sentences that followed as a commentary on their new first black attorney, I read the entire book thinking that the main character, Mitchell McDeere, was black. Here's the actual, unambiguous text: "He was white and the firm had never hired a black. They managed this by being secretive and clubbish and never soliciting job applications. Other firms solicited, and hired blacks. This firm had recruited, and remained, lily white. Plus the firm was in Memphis, of all places, and the top blacks had wanted New York or Washington, or Chicago."[1]

Of course there is no way I should have misread this. But once I missed the first three words of that sentence, I simply made everything else fit my too-easily gained impression that the text that followed was just a reinforcement of what an unusual hire Mitchell (as good a black name as any) was going to be for this firm. The text said: "Other firms had solicited"—and I read between the lines, "so why not this one?" Grisham wrote: "This firm had recruited and remained lily white"—and I read, "up until this time." And then: "The firm was in Memphis . . . and the top blacks had wanted New York or Washington"—I read, "but this young black attorney was smart enough to choose Memphis."

As I continued to read, I marveled at the skill and racial barriers that John Grisham was breaking. There was an occasional but not unexpected racial marker, for example, when his wife Abby was described as having long brown legs: "he stared at her long, brown legs. She wore a white cotton skirt, above the knees, and a white cotton button-down." Of course, she had been out in the Memphis sun, and Grisham had meant to signal she was tanned, but I read this as a permanent condition. This passage simply confirmed for me my reading of them as an African American couple. And I thought that, for a white writer, the author was handling this matter of race extraordinarily well.

The stylistic giveaway, in literature by black *and* white authors in the United States, is how and whether they describe the race of their characters. White authors invariably point to a character's ethnicity when they are not white. In their works, white characters generally go unmarked unless there is some direct interaction they are constructing with the other race—as Grisham had done in noting that Mitchell fit the requirements for a firm that had never hired a black attorney. African American or other people of color are described with markers that indicate their ethnicity—attention to their skin tone to signal their difference from the others, whose normative whiteness needs no description. Even Grisham uses this device to describe a character: "her dark curly hair was pulled back and hung almost to her waist. She was an exotic mixture of black, white, and probably Latin." And even though Grisham identifies Mitchell as white in that first clause I just breezed past, it was to point to the racial and gender practices of the firm that would make certain no one but a white attorney could be hired. Mitchell's racial identity began and ended with that sentence, but at later points in the novel, when someone is not white, Grisham makes certain that this difference is evident.

> They gathered each day for lunches prepared by Jessie Frances, a huge, temperamental old black woman.
> An angry black man with a red apron stood before them.

A courtly black man named Ellis delivered the menus.

Two large black men waited with a row of bulky cardboard boxes and an oriental rug.

A black boy grabbed Mitch's bags and threw them with Avery's into the trunk.

The first three rows were filled with elderly blacks.

It continues in exactly this fashion. No storyline necessity exists to identify these characters racially as black, just the habit that is characteristic of literature in the United States by white writers accompanied by a subtle implication that there are certain storied roles that seem best suited, for these authors, by a black person. In the excerpts I've noted, blacks occupy the position of three food service workers and two laborers. There seems to be no reason that they need these ethic markers. One might just have easily, it seems, been an angry man with a red apron or a temperamental old white woman, or even just a temperamental old woman. But the reasons that make these racially occupied and identified roles not as much a surprise as we might otherwise imagine is that they fit social stereotypes. And whether or not these social stereotypes find themselves appearing in a fiction seems to be a factor of who is writing.

In other words, you always know who is black in fiction by white folk. Or, you know who is not white. But in my misreading, I believed that Grisham had broken the mold, and this shift from the stereotype was remarkable. Once he described his main character Mitchell as a black man, he then just let it alone. Mitchell did not hang out with other black folk; he did not play black music; he did not go to black clubs or discuss race with black friends. There was no black church scene, nor was there argument or address by other partners or staff in the law firm about Mitchell's race. Grisham just noted the fact, and other than commenting on the color of Mitchell's wife's legs, he let it go. I thought this was a novel that broke the color line in fiction, and I was ready to herald the moment. But of course, I was wrong.

Reading race in literature is not only a complex engagement for contemporary writers; it has been a complicated business for two centuries. It has some relationship to how important it has been to distinguish between the races to maintain the privilege and protection of white America. The reason that literature about racial passing—black folks secretly crossing the color line into white America—in African American literature has nearly formed a subgenre within the tradition is because, for both races, the intrigue and the threat of racial passing have held considerable drama. It has been so important that in 1924 a black woman, Alice Jones Rhinelander, was the unprecedented winner in a lawsuit her husband and his family had launched against her, appealing for an annulment of their marriage because, the prosecution alleged, he could not have known she was black—she had duped her unwitting (or dim-witted, as the prosecution tried at first to claim) husband for the several months they were married. The case and trial are stunning because of the moment in the defense argument when her own attorney had her disrobe, from the waist up, to show her body to the jury of twelve white men—the implication being that her race would be apparent in the dark areola of her nipples. Had they ruled for the husband, these jurors would have advanced the dangerous notion that white men could be misled and did not have the essential knowledge to reliably detect the difference between the races. Whiteness could not be revealed as a fragile or a vulnerable assignment. Even though a black person winning a case in a courtroom against any white person is a rarity, this was especially true in the early decades of the century. In this case the matter on trial was discernment—and whites had to claim they could dependably determine what was a most basic and essential difference.

Mistaking a woman who is white as a black person slightly turns the tables, however. Whiteness had been the privileged spot. When those jurors gathered to determine whether Alice Rhinelander had confused her husband, the implicit text was whether she sought to claim, by subterfuge, the privilege that was theirs. This was the era when passing was spoken of in hush-mouthed family gatherings, when African Americans who were light skinned and nearly white in appearance slipped cross the color line, severing the bonds with their black families and communities. They lived as white folk ever wary of the potential for their unmasking by a chance recognition or the birth of a child whose skin was darker than the presumed parentage should have produced. The fear of this undercover racial posturing was enough to provoke family vows of silence. But to make an error the other way, removing someone from the white race and naming her as black, was a different matter entirely.

In 2005, when it was discovered that Emma Dunham Kelley-Hawkins, a writer that Henry Louis Gates included in the extraordinary forty-volume Schomburg Library of Nineteenth-Century Black Woman Writers series, was a white woman, the idea of a mistaken racial identity gained a bit of modern publicity. Kelley-Hawkins never wrote with the stylistic giveaway I discussed earlier: none of her characters was racially marked, other than being described as blond and pink complexioned. To some after-the-fact-was-revealed critics, this was sufficient grounds to question why a writer who was marked as a black author in this tradition would not have written about black folk.

When black authors write about white characters, they are as consistent as their white colleagues in marking the raced difference, and they mark these differences in similar ways. White characters are noted when there is an implied or actual comparison or contrast to the ways or means of black folks. In *Tar Baby* Toni Morrison's descriptors of white characters follow this convention: "Twice a year a professional maintenance crew came, four young men and an older one, all white"; or, "I tell you I can't pick up and move in with some strange new white folks at my age." James Baldwin's modifiers in *Go Tell It on the Mountain* follow a similar pattern: "he nearly knocked down an old white man"; or, "She was content to stay in this cabin and do washing for white folks." In black literature, tension between whites and blacks often plays a substantial role in the story. Instead of Grisham's casual notations, whiteness is marked as a formal distinction to what might have been the condition or experience of blacks. Only some black authors have written against this trend, notably Frank Yerby, Alice Walker, and Zora Neale Hurston.

In 1948 Zora Neale Hurston deliberately published a novel with whites as main characters. *Seraph on the Suwanee* was advertised and promoted to call attention to this uncommon device. However, despite her efforts to displace race, Hurston cannot avoid the characteristic signals in *Seraph* that betray her black authorship. When describing the main character she makes quite evident her identity—both in description and, in case that fails to inform, with the unmistakable labels that stand in for race: "She had plenty of long light yellow hair with a low wave to it and gulf blue eyes. . . . Arvay had a fine made kind of nose and mouth. . . . Arvay, young and white." Hurston's careful attention to the attributes of her character is one matter, but to position them as lead-ins to the statement that Arvay is white is a giveaway that the author is black. With this label, Hurston implicitly compares Arvay to the characters in her other novels, who were black.

For these reasons of style and form, Kelley-Hawkins was an enigma as a black writer. Using her novel *Four Girls at Cottage City,* published in 1898, it would have been easy to identify her as making the classic white author's gesture when she writes about her characters' decision to go to the theater even "if we do have to get seats in 'nigger heaven'" [2]—a name that marked the balcony seats blacks were restricted to during Jim Crow. This offense would likely have been handled differently by a black writer. But placing Kelley-Hawkins in the tradition of black writers with the understanding that she depicted whites without marking her main characters' race in any of her four novels made this unremarked-upon insult an oddity. Critics variously represented her characters as mulatto, or suggested that she buried race beneath her (admittedly thin) plots, or totally ignored the anomaly.

If authors like Hurston or Frank Yerby, as black writers, earned so much attention and focused critique for writing about white folks— what questions would have been appropriate to raise about Kelley-Hawkins, as an allegedly black writer, whose black characters would cast racial aspersions on themselves, or at least others of their race, without comment? One might at least pause over the appearance of this kind of careless and offensive epithet from a black writer—even when placed in the mouths of white characters. But questions like this one were not raised until Holly Taylor, a doctoral student at Brandeis

University, accomplished what appears to be a relatively uncompli-
cated genealogical search and revealed that the inclusion of Emma
Dunham Kelley-Hawkins in the black literary tradition was simply
wrong. Kelley-Hawkins was a white woman—and that fact explained
the racial lacunae in her writing.

Gates at first acknowledged his error in a rather inverted fashion: "I
am persuaded she was not black, and I welcome the finding," he told
the *Boston Globe,* when the research on Kelley-Hawkins was reported.

It is interesting to explore Henry Louis Gates's own history of
reading, included in his memoir *Colored People,* against both this misreading of Kelley-Hawkins and the ways in which he conforms to and
distinguishes himself from literati of the black tradition. The first difference is that he makes little effort to suggest that reading was a consuming passion for him as a youngster. For other writers of the century, reading voraciously and reading a sophisticated, "high culture"
literature early and often were ways to indicate they were destined
to and worthy of the roles they played as adults who were publicly
acknowledged as writers and intellectuals.

Gates, however, claims an early interest in a literature one might
characterize as being of lower cultural value when he remarks: "Oh,
I had read books before, mind you, and had read lots of them. But
sports books mostly." This is a strategic comment, because he makes
this confession to explain how he finally developed an interest in
the very books that would make his membership in that group of
twentieth-century black intellectuals and writers—although there is
a difference, even here. When he finally does make reading a priority,
it is not a mother's library or a father's urging that inspires him, nor is
it his own self-motivated intellectual curiosity. Gates's inspiration was
another student in his class in Piedmont, Virginia:

> If I was the school's prince, my princess was Linda Hoffman. It was in-
> evitable. Linda and I were the best students in our class. Linda and I
> were soulmates, or so I fantasized. She ate books. She read more books
> with more comprehension than anybody I knew. Total concentration
> was her gift. . . . She called me Gates, just like Momma called Daddy.[3]

To keep up with his "soulmate" is Gates's explanation and conflation of this relationship with the beginning of his habit of reading. He repeats some of the description offered earlier:

> I started to read that year, to bridge the gap with Linda. She was the one who ate books. She'd sit in study hall in total concentration, twirling her hair and devouring a book. So I started to read books, too. . . . Of course it wasn't just Linda's example that made me change. It was my teacher Mrs. Iverson who finally drew the line. Those books you are reporting on are fluff, she declared. You are forbidden to report on them anymore. Fluff? What was that? And what was I supposed to read instead? She gave me *A Tale of Two Cities*. I could never read a book that thick, I told her. Just read it, she said.

Gates begins his reading of a higher literary culture with Dickens and in this way finally joins other writers of the tradition when he marks his interaction with this author, who has been frequently mentioned by others in African American literary history. And, as is characteristic of the others, reading Dickens is eventually incorporated into a reading habit that includes serious and challenging books. Recall that James Weldon Johnson used Dickens to distinguish between the childish and elementary books that his father gave him and those more challenging works that he read alone or at his mother's urging.

At the point that writers mark the books they have read, we find either a list of authors, such as that of C. Eric Lincoln, or we find a certain selectivity and commentary, a blurb that contributes to the "reveal" in autobiography and memoir, and that suggests a carefulness in naming titles a reader can only link to the consistent authorial intent of the genre—to craft an image or to use a title to subtly signify something about the subject. Gates publishes this memoir seven years after publication of *The Signifying Monkey,* a book that won wide critical acclaim and academic notice. I think it interesting, at the very least, that the title of the one book he chooses to name, *Genius in the Jungle,* follows the publication of *The Signifying Monkey.* The full title of the biography he references on the list is *Albert Schweitzer: Genius in the Jungle.* But Gates leaves this identifying name of the biography's subject out of his memory of the book's title, retaining only the subtitle. A signifying gesture? One is left to wonder.

Gates is not the only black author to recall Schweitzer's biography. Claude Brown's *Manchild in the Promised Land* indicates the importance of that book for him as well, but he recalls the book in a conversation about how his life was changed by reading and the specific difference it made. Brown was explaining his detention in Warwick and how a teacher's gesture made the difference that distinguished him from those boys in Harlem whose stories would end up in adult prisons, and without hope.

> One day, Mrs. Cohen gave me a book. It was an autobiography of some woman by the name of Mary McLeod Bethune. . . . Before that, I had just read . . . trashy pocketbooks, stuff like *Duke: The Golden Spike,* that kind of nonsense. . . . I read it because I figured she might ask about it. . . . I felt that I knew something; I knew who Mary McLeod Bethune was. . . . Anyway, I felt a little smart afterward. Then Mrs. Cohen gave me other books, usually about people, outstanding people. She gave me a book on Jackie Robinson and on Sugar Ray Robinson. She gave me a book on Einstein and a book on Albert Schweitzer. . . . After reading about a lot of these people, I started getting ideas about life. . . . Then I read a book by Albert Schweitzer. He was another fascinating cat. The man knew so much. I really started wanting to know things, and I wanted to do things. . . . I kept reading, and I kept enjoying it.[4]

Brown's brief booklist names a genre that mattered to him, and the literature he read within that genre. Stories about others' lives made him both reflective and engaged, and changed the way he looked at his own potential. We know why the Schweitzer biography, and the others that he noted, mattered here.

The ways of reading these lists also allow us to discern how U.S. literatures mark race. When Gates writes about the reading he would share with Linda, the classmate who was his inspiration, we only learn her racial identity by inversion, the literary strategy that he spends a good deal of time exploring in *Signifying.* But we do learn it, and it does seem to matter. His readers come to understand that Linda is white by the book he offers to her as a (perhaps not so) subtle expression about his hopes for their relationship.

> I stayed up most of the night reading that book. . . . I went on to *Les Misérables,* to biographies of Einstein, then Schweitzer. I remember the green cover of *Genius in the Jungle,* by Joseph Gollumb. Schweitzer was a revelation. . . . I read *My Sweet Charlie,* a tearjerker about a black boy and a white girl who fall in love. He gets lynched, I think, or anyway something tragic happens to him because of white racism, and it all comes to a melodramatic ending. I gave it to Linda. I don't think she appreciated the plot.

My Sweet Charlie is a play by David Westheimer about a gifted and black New York attorney, wrongly accused of murder, who finds himself hiding out in a house also occupied by a poor, white, pregnant runaway, a southern girl whose meager education and lack of sophistication were part of the dramatic contrast between the two characters. I can't imagine Linda Hoffman appreciating the gesture.

Gates continues this exploration of his early reading and its contexts, writing:

> And then I read *The Agony and the Ecstasy,* completely enraptured by Irving Stone's divine kitsch. It was I who was carving the Carrara marble with my chisel as if it were clay. Best of all, though, was the passage about Michelangelo's making love with his mistress early in the afternoon, especially the part about how he had gone to her house unannounced, how she had answered the door clad only in a robe, which she opened for him when he kissed her, and how red her nipples appeared against her tanned body. I read that page so often, it started to turn yellow from exposure to the light. It was the first time I had been aroused by words on a page, a strange and magical experience. Only reluctantly did I return the book to the library.

Before Henry Louis Gates, James Weldon Johnson had been alone among writers of this tradition in noting books that encouraged a fleshly response. Johnson seemed to be encouraging the reader to align him with a tradition of arts and bohemia that would unabashedly claim the right to read erotica. Gates's discussion of Irving Stone's novel goes quite a bit further in describing his response to this work than does Johnson's somewhat more delicate indication that his reading of the "erotic" novels in the doctor's study left him "stirred and entertained."

In her essay "Uses of the Erotic" from *Sister Outsider,* Audre Lorde suggests that the erotic "forms a bridge between the sharers, which can be a basis of sharing what is not shared between them, and lessens the threat of their difference."[5] Lorde's is a provocative perspective from which to explore both Gates's and Johnson's engagement with some dimension of an erotic. Within her reading, both engagements, despite the difference in years that separates them, similarly situate an access point for their readers that might otherwise, because of differences in race, gender, or sexuality, seem untouchable. Lorde writes that when "in touch with the erotic I become less willing to accept powerlessness." In an important way, both Gates and Johnson engage and then claim a certain kind of authorial license with their engagement, not unrelated to Lorde's argument. Both writers confront a potential response that takes the autobiographical/memoiristic moment further than a booklist that may or may not appeal to a reader's intellectual interests. In their engagement with an erotic potential, they assert as well their *authority,* lending credence to Lorde's comments about the association between the erotic and power—and, in this case, engaging this relationship as an author and in an autobiographical moment. Gates's response to Irving Stone is detailed, unlike Johnson's near apologia (as sophisticated and as erudite it might be) for his own discussion. The difference may reflect the sixty-year span between the publications.

Gates's eventual engagement with reading marks an introduction to a higher literature than the sports books that heretofore had occupied him. Eventually he uses his reading list, like Marita Golden does, as a device to mark his racial coming of age. Gates explains that it was a priest at an Episcopal church camp in 1965 who gave him a book by a black author, a gift that shifts his self-awareness and that seems to mark as well a certain dimension of surprise (note the italicized *author* in the following excerpt, but *not* a racialized identification). Gates was drawn into the "sensibility" of Baldwin as a "black person," but he does not use the occasion of this textured analysis, a moment when his own writing takes on more scholarly formality than we see at other points in this memoir, to note that Baldwin named an experience that Gates might share. He maintains a certain and objective distance between the author and the book—it is "the American" cultural imagination that is named, not his own:

> A priest handed me a book. . . . From the cover, the wide-spaced eyes of a black man transfixed me. *Notes of a Native Son* the book was called, by James Baldwin. Was this man the *author,* I wondered, this man with a closely cropped "natural," with brown skin, splayed nostrils, and wide lips, so very Negro, so seemingly comfortable to be so?
>
> From the book's first few sentences, I was caught up thoroughly in the sensibility of another person—a black person. It was the first time I had heard a voice capturing the terrible exhilaration and anxiety of being a person of African descent in this country. The book performed for me the Adamic function of naming the complex racial dynamic of the American cultural imagination. I could not put it down.

Following this passage Gates, like Marita Golden, uses black authors' names, rather than titles or analysis, to signify a reading that would mark his coming into an age of civil rights politics and protest, when he and his friends formed "a black consciousness club. We began to read books together, black books, and to discuss them—Claude Brown, Eldridge Cleaver, Ralph Ellison, and Malcolm X."

A difference that emerges as significant in these booklists is the autonomy of selection—the ways in which writers indicate that they *chose* to read, or that they were inspired by their own curiosity and intellectual imagination to read, or that they were perspicacious enough to select a certain kind of reading that just happens to be among those designated as classics in the English literary tradition. Conversely, these narratives often indicate a distinction between personal choice and those books they were given to read. This is true for Gates, and he recounts the tale in a disarming and casual manner: he is *given* a classic by his schoolteacher that prompts his own latent literary curiosity and weans him away from sports, or by a priest who introduced him to black authors. But for another contemporary and prominent voice within black popular culture, the distinction between what a teacher prompts and what he selects seems warily strategic—carefully woven into the fabric of an essay that appeared as a "Bookend" in the *New York Times Book Review* and later in Michael Eric Dyson's *Between God and Gangsta Rap: Bearing Witness to Black Culture*.

That title itself forms the juxtaposition that finds its way into Dyson's booklist. A teacher, Mrs. James, "a honey-brown-skinned woman whose . . . sole mission was to bathe her students in the vast ocean of black intellectual and cultural life," was the source of his introduction to black cultural history, and it was Mrs. James who "accented the long history of multicultural America by emphasizing the contributions of black folk who loved excellence and who passionately and intelligently celebrated the genius of black culture." Mrs. James allows Dyson to introduce his own education in this tradition; she is his instructor and teacher. But notably, it is not Dyson who is the sole object of this attention and instruction but a collective "we": "We read about the exploits of black cowboys . . . studied great inventors like Jan Matseliger, Garrett Morgan and Granville T. Woods. . . . She told us of the debates between W.E.B. Du Bois and Booker T. Washington. . . . Mrs. James taught us . . . we would have to uphold the empowering intellectual and artistic traditions we were being taught."[6]

It might first seem only a happenstance of the autobiographical moment that the pronouns pronounced here are third person and collective ("she," "we," "us"). Dyson places himself fully within the company of his schoolmates. He relates this experience as a collective story about what this community of learners was taught by Mrs. James. It is a narrative technique that displaces the emphasis from the autobiographical "I" and, at first glimpse, seems a generous and inclusive gesture toward the whole of the community fortunate enough to be in her classroom. Even her race is not specifically named; we suspect she is a black teacher because of his description of her as "full-cheeked, honey-brown-skinned"—an adjectival cluster that seems to be more of an effort to describe a characteristic of her appearance as innocuous as her being "full-cheeked."

But I suspect this is not the case. Instead, Dyson makes evident her race in an indirect method that both gives him the opportunity and implies that it might not be his objective—but I think it is. And it is important to notice his use of inversion as Gates also uses the device, as a textual strategy—to pull the reader either away from or into a particular way of reading. Her race is not the issue at the moment. Instead, what she *taught* about race is the emphasis.

Michael Dyson's autobiographical essay continues in a way that is nearly a classic example of the manner in which these authors make either a direct claim to their elite literary training or acknowledge that they are the beneficiaries of someone else's generosity and inspiration. Recall that after a teacher gave the volume of Dickens to Henry Louis Gates, he became an avid reader of books that were more in that tradition rather than the sports stories that previously had comprised his literary interests. His acknowledgment of a black tradition does not appear until after he joins or forms a "black consciousness club." No book titles seem necessary here because the intent is to highlight blackness, not to elucidate its content.

Dyson's public posture, however, as a "hip-hop intellectual" seems to require more substantive engagement with the tradition, and Mrs. James becomes his key to this maneuver. Notably, it is not Dyson's singular or self-motivated interest that attunes him to the black text. He is one among his classmates who benefit from his teacher's initiative. Later his readers discover where his own curiosity led him and the emotional and intense response of the cultural tradition that evidently inspired him deeply.

Dyson names authors in the black cultural tradition, although a specific title only appears twice; otherwise we learn the names of authors and composers:

> She taught us the poetry of importance of Paul Laurence Dunbar, Langston Hughes and Margaret Walker Alexander . . . the importance

of Roland Hayes and Bessie Smith . . . Marian Anderson and Mahalia
Jackson . . . Paul Robeson and Louis Armstrong. . . . We were taught
to believe that the same musical genius that animated Scott Joplin
lighted as well on Stevie Wonder. We saw no essential division between "I Know Why the Caged Bird Sings" and "I Can't Get Next
to You."

Nowhere in this list is there any indication of an "I" or "my" voice. Indeed, no singular, first-person pronouns appear until its very end,
when Dyson makes a strategic shift from the names within a black
cultural tradition to the detailed and particularized classics of a European tradition. The shift is accompanied, or perhaps even announced,
by a dramatic change in voice: "Thus the post-modern came crash-
ing in on *me* before *I* gained sight of it in Derrida and Foucault" (my
emphasis).

At this narrative juncture, Dyson himself becomes the singular and
self-inspired subject. He relates how he was given a collection of
books by an *unnamed* widow of a "staunch Republican who had re-
cently died"—a collection that was first designated as a gift to "a local
library." His positioning regarding the source of his reading recalls
Malcolm X's insistence that it was the "Parkhurst collection" he read
from while in prison, a collection that any "college library" would
have been pleased to accept. In other words, its source marks an important distinctiveness. Dyson's notice of the Republican source functions in a way similar to Malcolm X's renaming the prison library
as the Parkhurst collection, and it is reminiscent as well of the persistent mention by C. Eric Lincoln of his northern resources. In case we
don't think the fact that the library belonged to someone very different from Dyson was important, he makes the point evident when
he includes a parenthetical comment that calls attention to the difference. Following the revelation that the husband and previous owner
of the "library" of books was a "staunch Republican," Dyson writes
that this was "a fact which, despite my own politics, cautions against
my wholesale reproach of the right." The parentheses give him a familiarity and nearness to a politic that would otherwise be very dif-

ferent from his. This comment, in isolation, might seem merely parenthetical. But when seen in company with these other writers in the tradition, who also distinguish themselves by creating a nearness to locales and resources that would not otherwise be theirs, it gains a strategic emphasis.

The absence of the donor's name stands in stark contrast to the generous and frequent credit and description given to Mrs. James and allows even more opportunity for Dyson to be alone and in his own company. Here, the authority of the booklist changes hands from a dedicated teacher with a mission to the hip-hop intellectual filled with courageous curiosity. He writes, "I was certainly the only boy on my block, and undoubtedly in my entire ghetto neighborhood who simultaneously devoured Motown's music and [from one of the Harvard Classics] Dana's 'Two Years before the Mast.'"

The singularity of his own curiosity, motivated by a gift of books that he alone chooses to "devour," is emphasized in the next sustained and detailed exploration and testament of his elite literariness:

> I can barely describe my joy in owning Charles Eliot's monumental assembly of the "world's great literature" as I waded, and often drowned, in the knowledge it offered. I memorized Tennyson's immortal closing lines from "Ulysses"
>
>> Tho much is taken, much abides; and tho
>> We are not now that strength which in old days
>> Moved earth and heaven, that which we are, we are,—
>> One equal temper of heroic hearts,
>> Made weak by time and fate, but strong in will
>> To strive, to seek, to find, and not to yield.

We read no similarly fondly remembered quotations from the black literati, and it seems that the selected quotation cannot be presumed to be casual. That is neither the purpose nor the effect of the autobiographical moment. Instead, it is meant to signify, and its selection suggests the way the writer wants the reader to receive and understand the history of self and substance that he offers.

Dyson writes that he is reading these Harvard Classics "in his early teens." With this in mind, the reader might be especially impressed with Dyson's intuitive gift, which comes at such an early age and gives him special insight into his own neighbors when he reads the British poets and perceptively marks a relationship between the images in that poetry and the situation of his peers:

> I cherished as well the sad beauty of Thomas Gray's poem "Elegy (Written in a Country Churchyard)," reading into one of its stanzas the expression of unrealized promise of children in my native Detroit:

> > Full many a gem of purest ray serene
> > The dark unfathom'd caves of ocean bear:
> > Full many a flower is born to blush unseen,
> > And waste its sweetness on the desert air.

As the lengthy list continues, marked with his own commentary and emotional response to some of the most commendable authors in English letters, it seems almost as if he is suddenly reminded of the positionality within a black tradition that might be the outcome of this autobiographical impulse. As if to return to that objective, he parenthetically inserts a gesture to an iconic figure, Martin Luther King. It is, nevertheless, a set of parentheses within a longer narrative:

> I pored over Benjamin Franklin's *Autobiography,* exulted in Marcus Aurelius; I drank in Milton's prose and followed Bunyan's *Pilgrim's Progress.* I read John Stuart Mill's political philosophy and read enthusiastically Carlyle's essays (in part because his words "No lie can live forever" were branded on my brain from repeated listening to Martin Luther King Jr.'s recorded speeches). I read Lincoln, Hobbes, and Plutarch; the metaphysical poets and Elizabethan drama. The Harvard Classics whetted my appetite for more learning and I was delighted to discover that it opened an exciting world to me, a world beyond the

buzz of bullets and whiplash of urban violence. One day, however, that learning led me right to the den of danger. Inspired by reading the English translation of Sartre's memoir of his childhood, "Les Mots" ("The Words") I rushed to the corner store to buy a cigar thinking that its exotic odor would provide a whiff of the Parisian café life where the aging master had hammered out his existential creed. . . . Just then I felt a jolt in my back; it was the barrel of a sawed-off shotgun and its owner ordered me and the other customers to find the floor. . . . Long before Marx and Gramsci would remind me, I understood that consciousness is shaped by the material realm, that learning takes place in a world of trouble.

True to both its intent and method, this sustained report concludes with an incident that marries the images of black and intellectual. On more than one occasion, Dyson calls attention to the danger that lurked in his neighborhood. His narrative vacillates between a black tradition that is the one Mrs. James illuminates as "empowering, intellectual and artistic" and another that haunts his surrounds—"the buzz of bullets and the whiplash of urban violence." The final story he tells here selects only one of these dimensions to intersect with the European intellectual tradition.

This extended passage, appearing both in the *New York Times Book Review* and in Dyson's book, is an exemplary indication of what a booklist accomplishes in the black tradition and of how strategically stylistic its composition might be. Although he claims a black location through his home in a "ghetto neighborhood," the peril he experienced there becomes a device to engage an extended narrative, allowing him to expose his immersion in a classic literature that he "pored over," "exulted in," "drank in," "read enthusiastically," and was "inspired by."

Because none of this emotionally powerful and affecting response seems attached to what he was "taught" or what he "read" or "studied" in the black tradition that Mrs. James brought to his awareness, and because of the imbalance of affect as they appear next to each other, the reader is left to understand that the weight of influence lies with those writers for whom he saves the extended quotations and elegant descriptors. Even though the last paragraph of the book review essay appears to bring together the two traditions in his "early habits of reading," the essay itself focuses on the differences between what he was taught by the "honey-brown-skinned" Mrs. James and what he selected to read from the library of the anonymous Republican benefactor. But most important is the last, curious sentence of the essay. The essay's intent seems to be to place cultures in contact and in balance—but what it accomplishes instead is to recall the pejorative imbrications of visual stereotype (pygmies) to an icon of high literary culture (Dostoyevsky) and to leave the readers of the *Book Review* with exactly that juxtaposition. I cannot believe that that was Dyson's intent, but it is nonetheless its impact:

> My early habits of reading are to me models of how the American canon can be made broad and deep enough to accommodate the complex meanings of American identity. To embrace Shakespeare, we need not malign Du Bois. To explore black identity, we need not forsake the learning of the majority culture. And even if a Dostoyevsky never appears among the pygmies, great culture may nonetheless be produced in unexpected spots.

One way to read and understand the role of booklists in this tradition is to distinguish between those authors who mention some combination of author, text, and title and then use that itemization to document and detail its consequence and those who simply list names of authors and consequentially allow the naming to carry its own significance. Does this difference convey interpretive significance or is it merely an effort to give a reading audience who might be unfamiliar with a text important to the writer more information about why a particular book was memorable? Does it mark a passage in a writer's life, or might it mark an identity? What we can be certain of is the distinction between these kinds of markings. One has a decided and likely specificity and the other seems merely an annotation. When, as in C. Eric Lincoln's *Coming Through the Fire,* we find an exhaustive list of authors (only), it is probably less important to note the specific names than the collocated set and what it symbolizes, including the way in which the outsider-at-the-end disrupts the list's internal coherence. And it is exactly at those points, when race seems a surprise, that it is worthy of some attention. It is also reasonable to consider that we might miss, when reading for race or reading racially, the texture of place, and the sensibilities and nuance of character that are not marks of identity but the residue of literary influence and knowledge.

Evidence of Kin

The error in the series of analyses, classifications, explanations, and yes, oversights that led to Emma Dunham Kelley-Hawkins's brief but textually confirmed sojourn as a black woman is in part evidence of our depending on the mark of race to be visible—and of our using that visibility to make judgments or to escape introspection that has no basis other than that specular mark of race. When the *Boston Globe* asked for his guess as to why anyone believed that Kelley-Hawkins was black, Gates offered what seems the simplest explanation. "I think it was the picture. . . . You put that picture up in my barbershop," Gates said, "and I guarantee the vote would be to make her a sister." The strategic shift in location here—from the meticulous research expected within the halls of the academy to an implicitly black neighborhood barbershop in which judgment about character and conduct is somewhat less formal—nicely illustrates the ways and means of racial identity in twentieth- and twenty-first-century America.

Race still matters enough that the kinds of conversations and meditations and repartee practiced in informal and yet insular community spaces contribute to the ways and means of our negotiations outside of those spaces. When a reader lays her hands on a text and a writer lifts her own away from it, finished with her part in the exchange and ready to release it to another, the negotiation of information that happens after that moment is not likely to be without error or imagination. As a matter of fact, that is often what writer and reader both depend on. Sometimes it is of little consequence, and other times it is deeply and strategically significant. In those moments, the exchange works precisely as literature should, urging a partnership between the book and its readers that allows something not entirely the reader's nor the author's to exist just long enough for the act of reading to occur. These are the earned and anticipated spaces of a fiction. Autobiography and memoir, however, are different from this. When authors of nonfiction place titles or authors or text into these narratives about their own bodies, it is both reasonable and appropriate to read these as signals of a certain sensibility or marks of a particular interest or identity. These are times when it makes good sense to anticipate that race does indeed matter.

ॐ

My mother shared my interest in reading books by Robin Cook and John Grisham. We both read rapidly, and we'd send these authors' books back and forth between our homes almost as soon as we'd get them, that is, unless I left them in the seat pocket of the airplane. They were dependably quick and absorbing reads for both of us, even though we didn't invest the time and attention we might have given another writer (but I make an exception here for Grisham's *The Painted House,* an exquisitely written novel that does not follow the patterns readers have come to anticipate from his legal fiction).

What I thought was John Grisham's racial breakthrough fell apart at a crucial point in the novel. Here, I was reading a bit more carefully. When the undercover activities of Mitch's wife, Abby, are about to be discovered, he desperately gives her some advice about how not to be noticed:

> "You've got to be careful. After dark, try to sneak into a drug store and buy some hair dye. Cut your hair extremely short and dye it blond."
> "Blond!"
> "Or red. I don't give a damn."

I'm reading—well he should give a damn. How in heaven's name would Abby, a black woman, be less noticeable with blond hair? This was the moment when Grisham's racial breakthrough broke apart for me. And after such a remarkable effort, I thought.

So when I shared my hilarity with my mother over how racially wrong Grisham got his character Mitchell McDeere, exposing the way in which racial knowledge can't just be invented like a fiction, I expected a shared laugh over Grisham's error that black folk might mask as blondes to pull off a caper without attracting much attention. My mother was perplexed. What makes you think Mitchell was black? She asked me in a quizzical way that opened the door to my first level of doubt, but one that indicated she was still willing to give me an opportunity to explain something she might have missed. She was generous like that. Well it says so on the first page. Are you sure? She asked in that gentle voice when I'm about to be proven wrong. I turned to the first page of *The Firm*. And there, clear as day, as my grandmother would say, I saw the words I had missed: "He was white and the firm had never hired a black." We had a good laugh over that one, and she, of course, made certain I remembered it well past the event, and that it was shared on as many occasions as seemed appropriate at family gatherings, especially because the constant complaint in my family is that I read too fast and that I can't possibly be taking it all in. I used to tell them I skip the conjunctions and prepositions—but now, I think they are likely right, I might want to pay closer attention to some of those nouns and adjectives.

10

The Card Catalog

Watching words develop their own world . . . I was entering the world through language.

RITA DOVE

I SPENT my high school study hall shelving books. I'd pile as many as I possibly could on the old wooden carts—the kind with the divider in the middle so that you could place a stack of books on each side. I would select the books to shelve that would allow me to gradually work my way to the back of the library. It was both escape and sanctuary.

I took the job as an alternative to an assigned study hall and as a way of gaining unfettered entrance to the library. And I did this even though the librarian at Bennett High School was one of the most acerbic and discouraging persons I have ever met. She stood behind the student workers at the counter where the library monitors were to collect and count fines as if she wanted to add her own two cents of vitriol to the wayward students who had been called to dole out their nickels and pennies by her demanding notes to their homeroom teachers. They would come in sheepish and reluctant, pay their fines, leave their delinquent books, and depart as quickly as they possibly could. I think her goal might have been to have as few students there to disturb her as possible—she made it such an unpleasant experience. I used to feel sorry for the students who had to use the library for an assignment or project; they would sit at one of the oak tables, shushed into perpetual silence, trying to tiptoe from the card catalog to one bookshelf and then another so as to attract as little attention as possible and certainly not any attention at all from the librarian, who could glower across the room in a way that would discourage even the most diligent of students. But there were a few of us courageous or crazy enough to volunteer as library monitors. We all had our reasons. Mine was that I liked to shelve books.

The allure of that small industry of shelving made me endure the militaristic patrol of the librarian. She spent most of the time monitoring the doors—so that she could repeat to all who entered the rules: silence; no pens, only pencils (so we would not inadvertently mark in the books); and the implicit rule of business, no pleasure. So she rarely made it to the back, where the fiction lined the far wall, and where I would spend my assigned period shelving. Then, and now, shelving books is my secret passion, and I was not about to give it up because the librarian was a curmudgeon.

If I didn't have enough books to shelve to last the entire period, I'd be called up to the return desk and made to take fines. Once in a while, after the lines of cowed students had been exhausted, and every penny wrung out of them before the next rush of students, the librarian would return to her desk behind the counter, and I was left there by myself. Then my job would be to arrange the cards that came from the book backs into proper order in the file shelf. There, whoever had signed out a book—from whatever era of high school—was recorded forever on the book's pocket card. When the card was full, we stapled it to the previous one. The cards told the story of the book's borrowing history. And for each book, there was the reliable index in the card catalog. There your skill came in being able to flip through the indexes to find the one book you wanted in the midst of the hundreds of cards held too precariously, it seemed, by the metal rod that joined book to book, author to author. You were always especially cautious when it became necessary to remove the entire file from its alcove in the cabinet and to place it onto the too-thin wooden trays that pulled out and separated the top rows of the rectangular wooden cases from those on the bottom. And even after you had successfully achieved this feat, you then had to return the file to its place among the rows and columns of the cabinet—balancing the file with your palm on the bottom, the other hand holding the front of the tray, slipping it silently, as into a sleeve, restoring the order and visual wooden landscape of the card catalog.

Of Books and Benefactors

Despite this librarian's vituperative demeanor, there is something that recalled her to me the first time I read Zora Neale Hurston's account of her encounter with the two ladies, Mrs. Johnstone and Miss Hurd, who, impressed with her classroom reading, gave Hurston her first books. These ladies were about as different from my librarian as I could imagine—except that each assured a place for books in a young-ster's memory that would last a lifetime. But the two "young" ladies Hurston writes about (my librarian was, at least to my high school eyes, old enough to be sitting on a rocker in a nursing home) gener-ously invited her to their hotel after hearing her read aloud the myth of Persephone in her classroom. "They took my picture under a palm tree" Hurston recalls in her 1942 autobiography, *Dust Tracks on a Road,* and the next day she received from them "an Episcopal hymn book bound in white leather . . . a copy of *The Swiss Family Robinson,* and a book of fairy tales." [1]

Throughout her life, Zora Neale Hurston's benefactors were to be some version of these white women. These first, among a series of "whites who came down from the north . . . brought by their friends to visit the village school," had an influence that was later matched by Hurston's literary patron and "godmother" Charlotte Mason, and later by her employer and likely literary nemesis, Fannie Hurst. All of these women, from the first two "long and thin, and very white" ladies who visited her classroom through to Hurst and Mason, would make a difference in terms of the books Hurston would read, write, or, in the case of Fannie Hurst's racial novel of passing, *Imitation of Life,* inspire. Her descriptions of the encounters she had with each of them are crafted with a careful attention that underscores her own extraordinariness and in that way matches the pattern of the tradition seen in other writers of the century. This first encounter with white women seems to set the narrative stage for the rest. She is in elemen-tary school when she meets Johnstone and Hurd, and even after they left Eatonville for their homes in Minnesota, Hurston writes, "they sent me a huge box packed with clothes and books." Dressed in her "not new, but very good" clothing, Hurston writes that she "shone like the morning sun," and then she describes the books from the box:

> In that box was Gulliver's Travels, Grimm's Fairy Tales, Dick Whit-
> tington, Greek and Roman Myths, and best of all, Norse Tales. Why
> did the Norse tales strike so deeply into my soul? I do not know, but

they did. I seemed to remember seeing Thor swing his mighty short-handled hammer as he sped across the sky in rumbling thunder. . . . The great and good Odin, who went down to the well of knowledge. . . . They held majesty for me. Of the Greeks, Hercules moved me the most. I followed him eagerly on his tasks. . . . I resolved to be like him. The tricks and turns of the other Gods and Goddesses left me cold. There were other thin books about this and that sweet and gentle little girl who gave up her heart to Christ and good works. Almost always they died from it, preaching as they passed. I was utterly indifferent to their deaths. In the first place I could not conceive of death, and in the next place they never had any funerals that amounted to a hill of beans, so I didn't care how soon they rolled up their big, soulful, blue eyes and kicked the bucket. They had no meat on their bones. But I also met Hans Andersen and Robert Louis Stevenson. They seemed to know what I wanted to hear and said it in a way that tingled me. Just a little below these friends was Rudyard Kipling in his Jungle Books.

Although Hurston's list is comparatively thinner than those of her contemporaries, it is thick with description and direction. There is no nuance in how her reader is instructed to think of this author—her comparisons and her preferences are made apparent. She chooses the powerful "majesty" of the Norse gods as her inspiration, the strength of Hercules as her model. She is patently uninterested in the books that were likely included here as a missionary appeal from the two visitors. She informs her reader that had these books about death and salvation included some attention to the cultural drama in traditions of funeralizing, they might have better captured her attention. She continues this discussion by pairing the impact of the myths with a story about her introduction to the Bible in a way that is especially telling, both in the nearness of one to the other and in the perspectives that this collection of myths and legends—biblical, Greek, and Norse—leaves with the elementary school–aged Hurston.

I came to start reading the Bible through my mother. She gave me a licking one afternoon for repeating something I overheard a neighbor telling her. She locked me in her room . . . and the Bible was the only thing in there for me to read. I happened to open to the place were David was doing some mighty smiting, and I got interested. . . . So I read a great deal more in the Bible hunting for some more active people like David. Except for the beautiful language of Luke and Paul, the New Testament still plays a poor second to the Old Testament for me. The Jews had a God who laid about Him when they needed Him.

Her strategic location of the Bible in a discussion of other myths and legends explains any questions her reader might have about her faith and her perspective on Christianity. As a woman writer at a time when women's roles were still publicly tied to the home, hearth, and marriage, Hurston, in her autobiography, labors to articulate her disassociation from these stereotypes and her difference from them. Her slim list is deeply provocative in its association with power, authority, and strength as well as its disassociation and critique of traditional structures.

At the point where the reader might consider that Hurston's appreciation and identification with the spirits of the gods may also make her vulnerable to their more fleshly vices, Hurston moves to separate herself from the reach of the fantasies of the gods and cautiously approaches the subject of sexuality. Unlike Gates and her contemporary James Weldon Johnson, Hurston gestures toward the flesh, but she rarely engages what might have been her reader's curiosity on this matter. Her caution, like all things Hurstonian, does not appear to be circumspect. She intimates the physical in a way that seems more matter-of-fact than it actually is. She is deeply aware of the way in which she has been received in literary circles as somewhat of an iconoclast, and she knows she cannot avoid the subject. Her "engaged disengagement" that follows, nicely juxtaposed in a sentence that includes a reference to her having read the Bible, is characteristically creative and fine, as she suggests that her education in things literary and spiritual included just a glimpse of the carnal but that there was nothing substantive in that kind of text to merit her interest or much more than brief mention:

Having finished [the Bible] and scanned the Doctor Book, which my mother thought she had hidden securely from my eyes, I read all the things which children write on privy-house walls. Therefore, I lost my taste for pornographic literature. I think that the people who love it, got cheated in the matter of privy-houses when they were children. In a way this early reading gave me great anguish through all my childhood and adolescence. My soul was with the gods and my body in the village.

Unlike some of her literary contemporaries, Hurston presents a list that is comparatively shorter—but she uses these authors as a way to give her reader a far more detailed image of herself. It is a method that she uses throughout the autobiography, remarking on a certain book or author, juxtaposing herself with or against them, and using the occasion to call attention, once again, to her iconoclasm. After explaining the strange "visions" that she asserts gave her a "knowledge before its time," she links herself to the writers she read, claiming a fellowship others might have challenged: "Kipling knew the feeling for himself, for he wrote of it very definitely in his *Plain Tales from the Hills*. So I took comfort in knowing that [we] were fellow pilgrims on a strange road."

Hurston's habit seemed to be to note her familiarity with books in a manner a bit like name dropping. Apart from the actual list that appears early in the autobiography, she casually drops selected titles throughout *Dust Tracks,* and in each example she rescues, retrieves, and is blessed with a perception that calls attention to her spirited intelligence and drive: "In a pile of rubbish I found a copy of Milton's complete works. The back was gone and the book was yellowed. But it was all there. So I read *Paradise Lost* and luxuriated in Milton's syllables and rhythms without every having heard that Milton was one of the greatest poets of the world. I read it because I liked it." This last sentence, "I read it because I liked it," reads like a retort to an unasked but potential question and as a way to make certain that readers understand that this choice of reading was no assignment, nor was it a gift. Later she writes of living with the family of a white clergyman while a student in the high school department of Morgan College, and it was in their home where she took advantage of their "great library":

> I waded in. I acted as if the books would run away. I remember com-
> mitting to memory Gray's *Elegy in a Country Churchyard* overnight,
> lest I never get a chance to read it again. Next I learned *The Ballad
> of Reading Gaol* and started on the *Rubaiyat*. . . . I had hundreds of
> books under my skin already. Not selected reading, all of it. Some of it
> could be called trashy. I had been through Nick Carter, Horatio Alger,
> Bertha M. Clay and the whole slew of dime novelists in addition to
> some really constructive reading. I do not regret the trash. It has
> harmed me in no way.

Again she writes as if responding to an unvoiced critique—ever cautious and always in control of an answer to even the potential question. Either Hurston is not confident enough to leave any speculation to her reader, or she is cautious enough to claim this control for herself. It takes some time getting into this autobiography before she delivers the traditional booklist. When she finally does, it is in the context of imagining herself as an English teacher—and here we get a sense of what she has absorbed through her education; what she feels competent to share; and through her sense of familiarity with the classics, which of these have been so important to make apparent for other authors within the tradition of African American letters:

> I decided that I must be an English teacher and lean over my desk and
> discourse on the 18th century poets, and explain the roots of the mod-
> ern novel. Children just getting born were going to hear about Ad-
> dison, Poe, de Quincey, Steele, Coleridge, Keats and Shelley from
> me, leaning nonchalantly over my desk. Defoe, Burns, Swift, Milton
> and Scott were going to be sympathetically, but adequately explained,
> with just that suspicion of a smile now and then before I returned to
> my notes.

It is not clear whether Hurston's suspicion of a smile was because she would likely not share with her students, if she knew it at all, that the Thomas De Quincey who makes it onto her booklist was most famous for his *Confessions of an Opium Eater*. It would not be unlike her to slip something like this into the midst of a serious list, to be writing for both text and subtext. But I suspect in this case it was not true, that instead she had reached the place in her life where her education mattered—her attendance at a school other than the little village school was available for scrutiny—and she was going to make certain that her education, and her knowledge about what books should be on the list of a good English curriculum and within the repertoire of a college graduate, would be apparent to her readers.

Hurston's brief consideration of her potential as an English teacher happens while she is a student at Howard University. Her teaching career amounted to little more than scattered and failed efforts, an outcome that some would argue today was a boon to students who might have been enrolled in her classes. She had neither the patience nor the temperament to conform to the regulations of any school system, and evidence exists of her failure to conform in her very brief forays in teaching drama. Nevertheless, this particular list is a commentary that marks the same kind of distance, albeit from a different direction, that W.E.B. Du Bois's booklists had for the "Negro Father" who wrote to him inquiring about which books he might add to his library and which books had inspired Du Bois himself. Hurston, who admits early in her biography that her "body was in the village" and her "mind was with the gods," seems to express a difference here that a reader might linger over. None of the books that inspired her imagination, none of the legends or the myths, and not even the Bible or fairy tales or any of the books sent in the box by the two visiting white ladies make it onto the list of books that might educate some future class of literature students. Here there is room only for the classics, which, book by book, from Kipling to Khayyám to Milton and Sir Walter Scott, were likely all from the Haldeman-Julius blue book reprints. Hurston has added to her own booklist, preparing her readers to accept as credible the implied erudition in her authorship.

A Scholar's Library

Hurston, however, was not a professor—nor could she be in the tradition, for example, of one of her contemporaries, J. Saunders Redding. Redding published his autobiography, *No Day of Triumph,* in the same year that *Dust Tracks* came out, and he left his professorship at Elizabeth City State University to become a professor at Howard University, the institution that Hurston's *Dust Tracks* labeled the "Capstone of Negro Education" and that prompts her own consideration of the professoriate.

Redding too uses the occasion of the autobiography to compile a list of books that played a role in his childhood education, but his is a curiously eclectic list that notably includes books both "read and recited *and hated* and loved" (my emphasis). But for one exception, his list seems familiar in its reach to the fantasy of childhood books and the then classic work by Booker T. Washington that marked the age of this generation of blacks in America. Redding's list included "fairy tales, *Up From Slavery, Leaves of Grass, Scaramouche, Othello, The Yoke, Uncle Tom's Cabin, The Heroic Story of the Negro in the Spanish-American War, The Leopard's Spots, Door of the Night, Sentimental Tommy, The Negro, Man or Beast?* and the rolling apostrophes of the *World's Best Orations.*"[2]

Redding's specific mention of Shakespeare includes a Moor—and is one way to understand that he was consciously, and without apology, creating a list that might represent an African American's reading and education in exactly the way that so many other writers of the twentieth century directly avoided. The list also includes some of the most offensive writing of the era—Thomas Dixon's *The Leopard's Spots* and Charles Carroll's *The Negro, a Beast, or, In the Image of God.* Dixon, author of the much reviled *Birth of a Nation,* wrote *Leopard's Spots* in part as a response to the "canonized" Negro in the other book Redding recalls, *Uncle Tom's Cabin.* In Dixon's novel, the hero is the

Klan, which protects the community from any "attempt to reverse the order of nature, turn society upside down, and make a thick-lipped, flat-nosed negro but yesterday taken from the jungle, the ruler of the proudest and strongest race of men evolved in two thousand years of history."[3] Charles Carroll's book is a deeply repugnant and therefore remarkable text for Redding to include in his booklist. It certainly marks a particular breadth and, in its unique insertion, is a deliberate intervention in a habit of marking books that were positively influential, important, or noteworthy. Its inclusion merits a closer look at Carroll's treatise, which, through illustration and text, offers an argument by which whites might better understand the distinction between themselves and "the Negro and other Beasts," as the title of its first chapter explains.

Whether Redding was deliberately naming a book he assumes is familiar to other writers in this tradition is unclear, since none of the others mentions, even in passing, books that have such racially invidious texts. It seems unlikely, though, that they would not know of these books. D. W. Griffith's film of Dixon's book was the subject of focused protests and strategic interventions by black communities and organizations. It is reasonable to suspect that Redding's list differs from others in this critical matter because his is a scholar's list — one for whom knowing a *full* complement of race literature is crucial to claiming a complete education. In distinction from that of his contemporary Zora Neale Hurston, Redding's list also performs a more racialized function—speaking outward to his audience about the kinds of experiences that shaped an African American consciousness and that must be engaged when talking back to the traditions in American letters.

There are at least two occasions when prominent spokespersons addressed the subject of how "Negroes" are portrayed in American literature. Both occasions were speeches delivered by women, and both occurred before the turn of the nineteenth century. Anna Julia Cooper's 1892 address critiquing disparaging images of blacks was titled "The Negro as Presented in American Literature"; three years later, Victoria Earle Matthews's speech to the First Congress of

Colored Women was titled "The Value of Race Literature." Redding, likely aware of this history, uses his booklist to imply that the formation of one literature, or even library, cannot fully explicate the situation and context of writing or reading about black or white folk without examining the social spaces in which these literatures are formulated, whether the portraiture is positive or offensive. Race literature was a vehicle to educate predominantly white audiences about the racism of the era. Redding writes with a highly stylized prose that showcases his command of literary device and manner as well—a habit I admit that I both recognize and resemble. His booklist falls within a discussion of what made an impact on him in his youth and conveys the atmosphere of the street in a way that foreshadows Dyson's memory of his own childhood neighborhood. But unlike Dyson, Redding, using the black classic sermonic style of narrative repetition, indicates that his education has meant his full embrace of the contradictions rather than his distance from one side or nearness to the other. As if to underscore the source of his rhetoric, he writes of the "spiritual side" of the struggle between two sides of the street— the "well-being of the west side and the grinding poverty of the east" —a contrast to the stark North–South divide and allegiances found in fellow writers.

> It was memory and history. . . . It was east side, west side, the white and the black, the word nigger. . . . It was Paul Dunbar whose great brooding eyes spirit-flowed from his drawn face in a photograph over our mantel. It was sleeping and waking. It was a science teacher saying . . . here I am teaching a school full of niggers. . . . It was the music of pianolas played from dusk to dawn. And it was books read and recited, hated and loved.

In an eclectic list of contrasts like this, and in a list that engaged the racism of the era of his youth, its black history, its traditions of oration, children's literature like J. M. Barrie's *Sentimental Tommy,* and fairy tales, J. Saunders Redding composes the only list in this history of bookmarks that might both explain a history of African American reading and imply that there are images in U.S. literature that are offensive to black folk. The eclecticism within this list is left to speak for itself, but he signals its tension by noting that, regarding the offensive literature and imagery, "on this plane allegiances were confused, divided."

Perhaps it is through this brief but decidedly complicated list made by a literature professor that we might better understand Zora Neale Hurston and so many other writers of this era as they both engage and disengage from racialized reading and as they embrace and distinguish themselves from literature's traditions. As a scholar and a teacher, Redding explained through his booklist the racial responsibilities and challenges of the nation's reading. Others for whom the *public* persona mattered more used the booklist to help their white readers mark them as a certain kind of African American—iconoclastic, erudite, traditionally trained, humble, assertive, or extraordinarily qualified. The books they listed may have the consequence of marking them as the exception in a country whose social history would ordinarily be poised to discount, or undervalue, the judgment and capabilities of its black citizens.

Common Texts

The writers and scholars who have taken the time to consider and use the opportunity of autobiography and memoir to record which books have mattered in their adolescent and preprofessional lives do not only leave evidence of what mix of literature has informed them, but they also deliberately signal to their readers the instructions and guidelines they want used in a reader's evaluation of their adult identities. It is not difficult, given the effort and attention black writers have directed toward this effort, to understand that the audiences they imagined as their readers were white. And for this reason in particular they labored to indicate the bookish authority that brought them to the moment of memoir, autobiography, or even interview.

Writers in African American letters have made common bedfellows of Haldeman-Julius books, the Harvard Classics, Charles

Dickens, the poetry of Paul Laurence Dunbar and James Weldon Johnson, English literature classics, and, for some, even comic books. According to these lists, all might seem equally as memorable. But this eclecticism argues instead for a purposeful, focused, and coherent trend among these literati, despite the generations, gender, and professions that distinguish them. The lists indicate the common ways and the racialized ways that they have learned to shape a language. These notations, their bookmarks, locate and authorize a professional expression. The common texts are not those within the African American literary tradition, nor are they the casual and informal reading of children. It is as important to notice that the booklists of African American literati are *not* full of the books "by and about Negroes" that W.E.B. Du Bois was to recommend in 1931 to the "Negro Father" as it is to understand and to consider that absence. The systems and values that have educated these literati have been those available to all students in public and private U.S. schools. The educations received in these schools by American writers of the twentieth century are no different from those received by any citizen. We have had a common corpus of what would compose a literate reader.

But our specific cultural literacy has also mattered. Whether that literacy came in adolescence rather than childhood, or through the care and attention of a culture-keeper—those race men and race women who preserved and passed on the aesthetics of African America—the fact is that it is evident in each writer's public profile, if not in the writer's booklists. These writers have shaped their professional identities with an intimacy and a deliberation that would match the culture-keeper's legacy. Sometimes the lists allow us to appreciate how cautiously that construction has occurred.

Writing autobiography and memoir is a self-conscious enterprise accomplished at the moment when the writer already occupies a certain adult identity. For these writers, that identity has been socially as well as self-consciously racialized. All of these writers have made race their subject—the *materia* of their teaching and lecturing, and the substance of their professional contributions. And each has written in an era—whether early, mid-, or late twentieth century—when

U.S. social and political structures reinforced the interpretive and consequential valence of race and its hierarchies. So when these writers, anticipating the racial difference between themselves and their audience, write about what they have read; or when we find an absence of race in that booklist; or when books that one might have expected would shape a racialized professional presence are tagged onto the end of a list or are listed so minimally as to seem insignificant, the absence begs interrogation. Is it a happenstance of their youth and schooling or a construction of their maturity? Is it an acknowledgment of the significance of racial identities that are out of their control or an indication that the common literature of U.S. education is theirs as well and does not discourage the specificity of a racial gaze developing as an adult occupation? What do the books that they recall to these formal and public moments of autobiography and memoir accomplish? How do they matter?

Although I had anticipated that my explorations would reveal that writers who focused on race in their professional or scholarly lives would have acknowledged a substantial impact from the fiction and nonfiction of the twentieth century that explored and imagined the ways in which race matters, *BookMarks* has uncovered a tradition of black writers' reading that is both similar to and different from this. For most of these writers, the way to mark their uniqueness, education, and competence seemed to be to call attention to their immersion in a literature that is best identified as classic within the English- and European-language traditions. To better understand this, it may be helpful to consider two final booklists and one public figure.

Octavia Butler and Samuel Delany are both contemporary African American writers who create fictions far afield from the specifically racialized focus that has occupied both the fiction as well as the nonfiction of other writers that are reviewed in this book. And even though there are absolutely dimensions of race and identity important to both Butler and Delany that emerge as distinctive in their fiction, the two authors focus primarily on an extraordinary version of the imaginary. Both of these writers of science fiction have had occasion to explain their evolution into writers of a certain genre within fiction, and their booklists testify to that effort. Octavia Butler recalled to an interviewer her foray into comic books, noting that "from the 60s through the early 70s I was very much into comic books —the Superman DC comic books first, then Marvel, and so on. I went around to all the secondhand stores and bought up the back issues as fast as I could."[4] Her readers understand that she expects us to note this as evidence of an early interest in things fanciful and extraordinary.

Finding that Butler shared the same habit as Rita Dove does not mean that we read the reports of this habit in the same way. Dove used the moment simply to prove that she read everything—even comic books. Her purpose was to indicate that the act of reading was its own objective, and this is what her repetition signifies when she recalls that "what I remember most about my childhood was curling up in a corner reading, reading, and reading. In the summer that was the thing I did. That was the thing I did to fill those long, boring days. . . . My first love was reading, and it took me to different worlds."[5] There is nothing about race she wants to indicate here; but there is something about her wide, uncensored, and full evidence of reading that this point was to document. The *habit* is her emphasis and objective.

Octavia Butler indicated how her adolescent reading presaged her adult occupation, her interest in things supraordinary. Her list assists and reinforces her adult identity as a writer of science fiction and fantasy. But she also acknowledges an important interest in an audience, recalling that she would "go down to the Salvation Army bookstore and buy copies of [Zenna Henderson's] *Pilgrimage* because I wanted someone to talk to about the book." I believe that her expressed interest in audience is the clue to the objective of those other writers in African American letters who compose these booklists.

In search of an audience and conversation, and with attention to the judgment a white reading audience might formulate, authors of these booklists anticipate a reader who would not find the kind of books Du Bois includes in his letter to the father as impressive as the classic European literature that Fauset located in her "attic." Notably, when Butler does follow the tradition of black letters and shares her booklist, the writers on it are from the genre that she comes to claim as her own. Even though she has been asked specifically what kinds of "SF" she read when "growing up," her response falls fully into the tradition of *BookMarks* as it details her reading and reveals as well what came before her interests in science fiction as well as what was her first interest after being liberated from the Peter Pan room in the children's library:

> Before I got into SF I read a lot of horse stories, and before that fairy tales. For some reason I didn't read Asimov until later, but I did read Heinlein and the Winston juveniles (with those fantastic inside pictures of all sorts of wonderful things that never happened in the book). Whenever I could afford them I'd buy copies of *Amazing* and *Fantastic*. . . . After I got out of the Peter Pan Room, the first writer I latched onto was Zenna Henderson, who wrote about telepathy and other things I was interested in, from the point of view of young women. . . . I read all of Marion Zimmer Bradley's Darkover books. I especially liked Ursula Le Guin's *Dispossessed,* and the original *Dune* by Frank Herbert was another favorite of mine. I read Harlan Ellison's stories and also John Wyndham, Arthur C. Clarke, A. E. Vogt, Isaac Asimov —all the SF classics, whatever I got my hands on.

As if to corroborate the difference that science fiction makes and the way in which a list articulates identity, Samuel Delany composes a booklist that, like Butler's, lists books that helped him to imagine and formulate fantasy—images that would become important to his adult subject. Delany recalls memorizing in elementary school "The Raven" and "Jabberwocky" and Gilbert and Sullivan lyrics. He learned

> long slabs of *A Midsummer Night's Dream* . . . and *The Waste Land,* and "The Love Song of J. Alfred Prufrock"—because Sue-Sue, in the high school division, told me Eliot was impossible to understand and I'd

show them—and read science fiction with Robert and Johnny and borrowed Priscilla's *Mad* comic book to read in the boys john, cover to cover.[6]

As a young adult, Delany recalls that

> fiction itself was the series of overwhelming effects from works I'd read in adolescence: the torture scene in Heinlein's "Gulf"; the scene in Steinbeck's *The Grapes of Wrath* where, after endless and exhausting trails, the Joad family come upon the peace, cleanliness and community of the government migrant labor camp; Dr. O'Connor's "Watchman, What of the Night?" monologue in Barnes's *Nightwood*.

These two writers of science fiction, who mention nothing necessary about reading racially, seem to explain the construction of public identities that emerges in other writers. And importantly, their lists corroborate the collective impression left from the gathered writers who appear here, in *BookMarks*. Both Butler and Delany share lists that they see as representative of the person they have become. The difference is that these other writers make certain that their readers can appreciate them as extraordinarily competent and gifted *outside* of the racialized tradition so that their personae as men and women of African American letters are met with the credibility and authority extended to whites who have mastered the common texts. Lengthy lists of black books would not have assisted them as long as the judgments their white readers would make about conduct and character were constructed within a norm of education and accomplishment in which the public standard and common texts are more like those of Dickens than Du Bois.

Public Readers

A unique individual, and moment, might best illustrate how a public recitation of books is intimately attached to the bodies of black folk. Oprah Winfrey and Oprah's Book Club are perhaps the most striking illustration of how a public recitation of books can be an instrument of identity.

When Oprah's televised book club became a mainstay of her talk show at the end of the twentieth century, the public response was overwhelming and extraordinary. The publishing industry had found its public champion of books, and it exalted and cultivated the attention that a book selection by Oprah would mean for the business. Authors who found themselves the object of Oprah's attention faced an onslaught of media attention—and audience purchases. It would be enough to mark Oprah's Book Club as a late-century version of the booklists included in the memoirs and autobiographies written by African Americans and to note that since her talk show engages her life's story as its frequent frame, Winfrey has shifted the text only slightly —from script to screen. Oprah's book selections intimated that her audiences might learn something more about the person they craved to know. The selections and her conversations about them allowed another privileged moment as her viewers shared Oprah's "favorite books." But perhaps the most interesting moment of the phenomenon of Oprah's Book Club was the season that she turned to the "classics." Like the black authors who participate in this tradition, whose selective and thoughtful lists work to complicate, explain, and position their readers' understanding of them, Oprah Winfrey, in her turn to "great books," signaled to her wide audience that she too has read, can discern among, and can advise others with regard to literature's "classic" texts. If she was speaking back to critics who have been dismissive and skeptical of her bookishness, then this was the objective of a booklist. If she was advising her viewers that her young adult reading included "high-brow" authors, and that she did not "produce" this interest in classics solely for the television audience, then this was the purpose of a booklist. Winfrey actually made this point clear in an interview in *Life* magazine, in an article strategically titled "Oprah Winfrey: A Life in Books," when she explained to the interviewer that "she spent her twenties catching up on classics she missed in school saying 'I liked Hemingway. Steinbeck was my favorite.'"[7] And if we are to understand that Winfrey's life, and the authority and respect given to these classic writers might have a point of intersection, then her booklist-like move of selecting the classic "great books" made this mark as well.

Whether authors recall Dickens or Du Bois, whether they admit to an obsession with comic books or cowboy books or fairy tales, whether they find careers in science fiction or in the public domain, it is possible to recognize in their booklists the refined maneuvers, and ultimately the inescapable mark, of self-authorship. The autobiographical moment of a booklist is a way to be marked with the authority that books represent. And for black folk in America, this might mean an intimate relationship with a library of books that can contradict the stereotypes that a black life might engage.

Once I got to college, I found I owed thanks to both librarians of my youth, despite their differences from each other and my responses to them. I discovered that I was well acquainted with the operation of a library's inner and outer shells. I was privy as well to the mysteries of the card catalog and savored the secluded enjoyment of a library's spaces. But I knew nothing about how a history might be held and preserved within the space of a library. Our first campus tour as newly arrived freshmen at Talladega College ushered us through the revolving doors of Savery Library. We were quickly directed to move to either the left or the right and to avoid at all costs stepping onto the center of the floor. Once gathered in a respectful circle around the librarian, whose calm, interest, and welcome formed a distinct contrast to the high school librarian who was quickly fading from my memory, we all looked down to see what it was that we had so carefully avoided. I think that the way we circled that image on the floor, adding our frame to the image preserved there, was the beginning of our respectful relationship to the place. On the floor was a terrazzo mural of the slave ship *Amistad,* its soft sea colors of blue, white, and green delicately edged in brass—its motion suggested by the ship's billowing sails and the near relief of its impression bursting from the floor's speckled surround. The image immediately made apparent the unique importance of this space. As we circled the ship, we were told the absorbing story of the *Amistad* revolt in 1839. And then, at an appropriately dramatic moment in its telling, we were invited to look up. The brilliant murals of the mutiny and trial of the Africans on the *Amistad* were illustrated above. A triptych of the incident, painted by Hale Woodruff, covered the full expanse of the back entrance wall and depicted the major scenes in this historic narrative: the revolt on the ship, the courtroom trial, and the return of the Africans to their homeland. Woodruff's murals are bold and invigorating; the proud and courageous bodies of the enslaved Africans are sinuous, graceful, and marvelously colored. Talladega students know that the artist's own image is painted into the scene as one of the courtroom observers—testament that as an African American, he recognized his own place within this story. Implicitly we were invited to consider ourselves within that company.

So even before you get into Savery's sunlit main reading room to find your place at one of the long oak tables stretching down its expanse, and before you are invited to explore the aged iron shelves in the library's stacks, you learn the story of the *Amistad* murals. Then you are instructed to turn to see the old card catalog files against each of the far walls of the entrance. Their fine and well-used cabinetry extends from one side to the other. At that moment you are fully initiated into the history of the place, and you begin to understand that whatever work you might do there must be fine enough, in seriousness if not in quality, to be held within the tradition of this library and its archives of black education and freedom.

When I read Jamaica Kincaid's memoir of Antigua, *A Small Place*, the sensory memory of Savery Library returns. Kincaid writes:

> If you saw the old library, situated as it was . . . its big, always open windows, its rows and rows of shelves filled with books, its beautiful wooden tables and chairs for sitting and reading, if you could hear the sound of its quietness (for the quiet in this library was a sound in itself . . . the heat of the sun . . . the beauty of us sitting there like communicants at an altar, taking in, again and again.[8]

The Trial of the Captives, *a section of the* Amistad *triptych mural by Hale Woodruff. Photo courtesy of the Savery Library Archives, Talladega College, Talladega, Alabama.*

This sensory mark of a communicant is what remains from Talladega's Savery Library. Did my parents have this in mind when I was weighing a choice between Talladega and Bennington (two options whose difference I came to appreciate more in later years than in the senior year of high school, when it just seemed one was south, the other north)?

Perhaps. Any former student of the college, as were both of my parents, would have known that part of the allure and impact of the place had to do with the history of the race that it held as well as the responsibility to black education that was its mission. Savery Library holds its place as the final installment in whatever narrative could be constructed about the importance of the spaces of reading, and the books read, in African America. And if we want a record of these, we need only turn to the card catalog.

Epilogue

Pondering Color

And since she knew death was anything but forgetfulness, she used the little energy she had left her for pondering color.
"Bring a little lavender in, if you got any."

TONI MORRISON, *Beloved*

SOME years into my children's childhoods but well before their adolescence, my sister and their aunt Karen died. We were all stunned and deeply troubled, trying to make sense of the loss of this beautiful young mother, killed in a car accident just after having made application to the Episcopal postulancy. We were grief-stricken, and, as children will be, Ayana and Bem became especially worried about the whole matter of death, dying, and loss in this, their first intimate encounter with its anguish. In a moment that I think of now as an effort to assure them that there is some permanency beyond that which we easily imagine, I remember telling them, don't worry. Mom will live forever in the card catalog.

I don't know who was more surprised with the vitality that that assurance took on for them. At various events in our lives since, stunned by loss or impermanency, or just when we needed to be assured that there were ways and means more remote than those we might recall to any moment but that we nonetheless found unconditional and dependable, any one of us was likely to recall those eight words, an aphorism of their own making, made visible by our memories of our encounters and indeed romance with those bins full of weathered cards. The indentation and shadowy impress of typewriters too old for memory list book after book, and their authors, with the certainty that when we flipped past any one of those cards, the dry click being the only disruption to the arid silence in the library's stillness, there would always be so many more of them left than we would have days to discover.

Today, my bookshelves reflect the mix and method that have emerged from the orders, and the disorders, of my life. There is shelving by word. Books with the word "Harlem" in the title, or "race." There are rows of works written only by women or by men. Certainly there are books that are somewhat more traditionally organized by subject, like "British literature" or "linguistics" or "law." But my favorite shelves, those that feel most familiar, those that have been most carefully selected, are colored: blue greens fading to spare shades of azure and then to deeper tones—turquoise, sapphire, cerulean. There is a shelved series of red books and a black black book shelf. There is a shelf of sand-, taupe-, and ginger-colored, tawny books. These are just beneath the sea shelf—the ones with blues and greens. I still wish for more purple books—I imagine them as lavender and plum and even some deepened toward aubergine.

I know fully and well that this is no way to shelve books. Nevertheless, it is a way toward a contemplative space, a means of composing my days when I need a certain quiet and calm and an order of my own, considering color and using my books to mark its place.

Author Profiles

<u>Maya Angelou</u> (1928–)

Maya Angelou was born Marguerite Johnson on April 4, 1928, in St. Louis and spent her childhood years in rural Arkansas. She is an author, poet, actress, playwright, producer, and director. She lectures throughout the United States and internationally. Her books and numerous magazine articles have earned Pulitzer Prize and National Book Award nominations. Although Angelou began her career in drama and dance, later, when living in Cairo and then in Ghana, she worked as a journalist and taught at the University of Ghana. Her renowned autobiography, *I Know Why the Caged Bird Sings,* first published in 1970, is widely used in school curricula from junior high school through college throughout the United States. She is the author and producer of several prize-winning documentaries, including "Afro-Americans in the Arts," a PBS special for which she received the Golden Eagle Award. She was also nominated for an Emmy Award for her acting in the television adaptation of Alex Haley's *Roots.* She is currently Reynolds Professor at Wake Forest University, Winston-Salem, North Carolina.

<u>James Baldwin</u> (1924–1987)

James Arthur Baldwin was born in Harlem, New York City, August 2, 1924, and died on November 30, 1987. He was the eldest of nine children, and at the age of fourteen, at the urging of his stepfather who was a minister, Baldwin became a preacher at the small Fireside Pentecostal Church in Harlem. After he graduated from high school, he moved south to Greenwich Village, where his literary career was born. His first novel, *Go Tell It on the Mountain* (1953), is a semi-autobiographical reflection on his youth and adolescence. His essay collections, *Notes of a Native Son* (1955), *Nobody Knows My Name* (1961), and *The Fire Next Time* (1963), have been critical in cementing his reputation as a fierce intellectual voice that focused on civil rights.

Baldwin made his home primarily in the south of France, but he traveled and lived throughout Europe (especially Switzerland and Turkey) and often returned to the United States, especially to the American South during the era of civil rights protests. His novels include *Giovanni's Room* (1956) and *Another Country* (1962). *Blues for Mister Charlie,* a drama, was produced in 1964. The essay collections *Going to Meet the Man* (1965) and *Tell Me How Long the Train's Been Gone* (1968) continued his focus on American racism.

<u>Octavia Butler</u> (1947–2006)

Octavia Estelle Butler was born in Pasadena, California. Butler's passion for science fiction began early; by the time she was thirteen, she was writing and submitting her own stories to magazines. She received an Associate of Arts degree from Pasadena City College and attended California State University. She credits two writing workshops—the Open Door Program of the Screen Writers' Guild of America, and the Clarion Science Fiction Writers Workshop —as being particularly important to her writing. She is a prolific author of science fiction and fantasy, and has been recipient of the Hugo Award, Nebula Award, Locus Award, and the Science Fiction Chronicle Award. She has also been recognized with the prestigious MacArthur Foundation fellowship and has received a lifetime achievement award from PEN. Among her twelve novels are two series, the Patternists and Xenogenesis. Her books include *Wild Seed* (1980), *Kindred* (1988), *Lilith's Brood* (1989), *Bloodchild, and Other Stories* (1995), *Parable of the Sower* (1995), *Parable of the Talents* (1998), and *Fledgling: A Novel* (2005).

ELDRIDGE CLEAVER (1938–1998)

Leroy Eldridge Cleaver was born in Wabbeseka, Arkansas. His family later moved to Los Angeles, where he got into trouble as a teenager and was sent to prison for possession of marijuana. He was sentenced to thirty months in Soledad Prison. Although he was released in 1957, he was arrested the next year and charged with attempted murder and sentenced to a term of two to fourteen years in San Quentin Prison. After his release, he rose to prominence through his founding leadership of the Black Panthers in 1966 and as its minister of information. *Soul on Ice* (1968), a collection of essays from his prison years, received wide notice and acclaim upon its publication. The year of its publication, he was wounded in a Panther shootout with Oakland police. He fled to Algeria and lived in exile there and in Paris, returning to America in 1975. In his later years he became a born-again Christian and a conservative Republican—conversions he explored in *Soul on Fire* (1978).

ANGELA DAVIS (1946–)

Angela Yvonne Davis was born in Birmingham, Alabama. After graduating from high school in New York, she attended Brandeis University and studied abroad in Switzerland and Paris. Davis attended the University of Frankfurt for graduate studies in philosophy. Although away from the United States, she was deeply affected by U.S. national politics of the era, including the bombing of the church in Birmingham and the politics of the Vietnam War. Davis returned to California for her master's degree and then earned her doctorate from Humboldt University in Berlin. By then she had become a member of the Communist Party and had formed an association with the Black Panther Party. Both affiliations were politically explosive, and the latter one especially led to her being targeted by the FBI and arrested for alleged participation in an attempted prison escape during which a guard was shot with a gun registered in her name. She was imprisoned in the Women's Detention Center in New York—an episode that has contributed to her contemporary activism, especially in regard to prison abolition. Davis is currently a UC presidential chair and a professor in the history of consciousness department at UC Santa Cruz. Her published volumes include, in addition to her 1974 autobiography, *Women, Race, and Class* (1981), *Women, Race, and Politics* (1989), *Blues Legacies and Black Feminisms* (1999), and *Are Prisons Obsolete?* (2003).

SAMUEL DELANY (1942–)

Samuel Ray Delany was born in New York City, where he attended the Bronx High School of Science and the City College of New York. He published his first novel, *The Jewels of Aptor,* in 1962. His works include the trilogy titled *The Fall of the Towers* (1963) as well as *The Ballad of Beta-2* (1965) and *Babel-17* (1966). Delany won the science fiction Nebula Award for the latter work as well as for the subsequent *Einstein Intersection* (1967). He also received Nebula awards for "Aye, and Gomorrah" (1968) and *Time Considered as a Helix of Semi-Precious Stones* (1969). His critical writing includes *The Jewel-Hinged Jaw: Notes on the Language of Science Fiction* (1977) and *The American Shore* (1978), both of which earned him the Science Fiction Research Association's Pilgrim Award. The five books in his Neveryon series have earned him wide popularity. In 1988, he published an autobiographical memoir, *The Motion of Light in Water.* He is also the author of the novels *Dhalgren* (1975), *Triton* (1976), *They Fly at Ciron* (1993), and *The Mad Man* (1994). Samuel Delany accepted a teaching position at the University of Massachusetts at Amherst in 1988, where he is now a professor of comparative literature.

RITA DOVE (1952–)

Rita Dove was born in Akron, Ohio. She stayed in the Midwest to earn her bachelor's from Miami University of Ohio and her M.F.A. from the University of Iowa. Her poetry collections have included *The Yellow House on the Corner* (1980), *Museum* (1983), *Thomas and Beulah* (1986), *Grace Notes* (1989), *Selected Poems* (1993), *Mother Love* (1995), *On the Bus with Rosa Parks* (1999), and *American Smooth* (2004). She is also the author of a book of short stories, *Fifth Sunday* (1985), the novel *Through the Ivory Gate* (1992), essays collected under the title *The Poet's World* (1995), and the play *The Darker Face of the Earth,* which had its world premiere in 1996 at the Oregon Shakespeare Festival. From 1993 to 1995 she served as poet laureate of the United States and currently serves as poet laureate of the Commonwealth of Virginia. Among her literary honors is the 1987 Pulitzer Prize in poetry, the 1996 National Humanities Medal, and the 2001 Duke Ellington Lifetime Achievement Award. Dove has also held a Fulbright scholarship at the University of Tubingen in Germany. She currently holds the Commonwealth Professor of English chair at the University of Virginia.

W.E.B. DU BOIS (1868–1963)

William Edward Burghardt Du Bois was born in Great Barrington, Massachusetts. He received a bachelor's degree from Fisk University and went on to earn a second bachelor's, as well a Ph.D., from Harvard. He held teaching positions at Wilberforce, the University of Pennsylvania, and Atlanta

University. His teaching portfolio included courses in Latin, Greek, economics, and history. One of the founders of the National Association for the Advancement of Colored People (NAACP) in 1909, Du Bois served as that organization's director of publications and editor of the *Crisis* magazine until 1934. In 1961 he emigrated to Ghana and became editor-in-chief of the *Encyclopedia Africana,* with the cooperation and encouragement of Kwame Nkrumah. On the day of the March on Washington in the United States, August 27, 1963, it was announced to the gathered crowd that Dr. Du Bois had died in Ghana at the age of ninety-five. His numerous books represent an impressive array of genres and scholarship. They include history, poetry, sociology, fiction, as well as collections of essays: *The Suppression of the Slave Trade* (1896), *The Philadelphia Negro* (1899), *The Souls of Black Folk* (1903), *John Brown* (1909), *Quest of the Silver Fleece* (1911), *The Negro* (1915), *Darkwater* (1920), *The Gift of Black Folk* (1924), *Dark Princess* (1928), *Black Folk: Then and Now* (1939), *Dusk of Dawn* (1940), *Color and Democracy* (1945), *The World and Africa* (1947), *In Battle for Peace* (1952), and a trilogy, *Black Flame* (1957–1961).

Michael Eric Dyson (1958–)

Michael Eric Dyson was born in Detroit, Michigan. He earned a bachelor's degree from Carson-Newman College in Tennessee and his master's and doctoral degrees from Princeton University. In addition to being a scholar and teacher, Dyson is an ordained Baptist minister. He moved to his current position as Avalon Foundation Professor in the Humanities at the University of Pennsylvania from DePaul University. He is the author of seven books, including *Race Rules: Navigating the Color Line* (1997), *Between God and Gangsta Rap: Navigating the Color Line* (1997), *I May Not Get There with You: The True Martin Luther King Jr.* (2001), *Holler If You Hear Me: Searching for Tupac Shakur* (2001), and *Is Bill Cosby Right? Or Has the Black Middle Class Lost its Mind?* (2005). Dyson's commentaries are heard regularly on National Public Radio.

Jessie Redmon Fauset (1882–1961)

Jessie Redmon Fauset, born in Snow Hill, New Jersey, was an essayist, editor, and novelist who rose to prominence during the Harlem Renaissance, especially because of her affiliation with the NAACP's journal the *Crisis*. She was both an editor and contributor to the magazine and the most prolific novelist of the age. Fauset completed high school in Philadelphia, then graduated with degrees from Cornell in 1905 and received a master's in French from the University of Pennsylvania. Fauset left the *Crisis* in 1927 to achieve a more ordered life as a French teacher at De Witt Clinton High School. She continued to teach in New York until 1944 and later taught as a visiting professor in the English department at Hampton Institute. Her novels include two about racial passing: *There Is Confusion* (1924) and *Plum Bun: A Novel without a Moral* (1928). In 1931 she published *The Chinaberry Tree: A Novel of American Life* and in 1933 *Comedy, American Style*.

Leon Forrest (1952–1999)

Leon Richard Forrest was born in Chicago and grew up in a middle-class neighborhood on Chicago's South Side. Although he began a course of study at the University of Chicago, he dropped out, was drafted, and spent a tour of duty in Germany, where he worked as a journalist and wrote drama when off duty. Forrest worked as a journalist and editor for several community newspapers and in 1969 joined the newspaper of the Black Muslims in America, *Muhammad Speaks,* eventually being promoted to its managing editor. He wrote and published four novels: *There Is a Tree More Ancient Than Eden* (1973), *The Bloodworth Orphans* (1977), *Divine Days* (1977), and *Two Wings to Veil My Face* (1984). A collection of more than a hundred essays, *Relocations of the Spirit,* was published in 1994. Forrest taught for twenty-four years at Northwestern University, where he served as chair as the African American studies department and taught courses in creative writing and African American literature. His fifth novel, *Meteor in the Madhouse,* was published posthumously in 2000.

John Hope Franklin (1915–)

John Hope Franklin was born in Rentiesville, Oklahoma, in 1915. His family relocated to Tulsa, Oklahoma, shortly after the Tulsa rebellion of 1921. Franklin received an A.B. from Fisk University in 1935 and his A.M. and Ph.D. degrees in history from Harvard University. His teaching career began at Fisk University, but he moved to North Carolina, where he taught at St. Augustine's College in Raleigh and what was then North Carolina College for Negroes in Durham. In 1945, with a $500 advance from Alfred A. Knopf, Franklin began writing the classic African American history text, *From Slavery to Freedom.* Franklin has taught at Howard University and Brooklyn College, and at the University of Chicago, where he chaired the Department of History. In 1982, Franklin joined the faculty at Duke University as the James B. Duke Professor Emeritus of History. He has been president of the Southern Historical Society, the Organization of American Historians, and the American Historical Association. In 1997, he was appointed by President Bill Clinton as chairman of the advisory board for One America, the President's Initiative on Race. President Clinton awarded Dr. Franklin the Presidential Medal of Freedom. Among his works are *The Free Negro in North Carolina* (1943), *Runaway Slaves: Rebels on the Plantations* with Loren Schweninger (1999), *Racial Equality in America* (1976), *George Washington Williams: A Biography* (1985), a book about his father titled *My Life and an Era: The Autobiography of Buck Colbert Franklin* (1998), and his autobiography, published in 2005, *Mirror to America.*

Henry Louis Gates Jr. (1950–)

Henry Louis Gates Jr. was born in Keyser, West Virginia, and grew up in Piedmont. He graduated from Yale University with a bachelor's degree in 1973 and took his master's and doctoral degree from Clare College of the University of Cambridge. He has established his scholarly expertise in African American literature, history, and culture and has brought several previously lost works back to the tradition of African American letters, including the first known novel by an African American, Harriet E. Wilson's *Our Nig* (1859). His books include *Figures in Black: Words, Signs, and the "Racial" Self* (1987), *The Signifying Monkey: A Theory of African-American Literary Criticism* (1988), *Loose Canons: Notes on the Culture Wars* (1992), *Colored People: A Memoir* (1994), *The Future of the Race* (1996), and *Thirteen Ways of Looking at a Black Man* (1997); he is coeditor of *The Dictionary of Global Culture* (1997). He was in the first class of MacArthur Foundation fellows and has received a host of honors and awards during his professional career, including being named one of *Time* magazine's "25 Most Influential Americans." In 1999 he wrote and hosted a public television series on Africa and published *Wonders of the African World*. Gates is former head of the Afro-American Studies department at Harvard University and a member of the American Academy of Arts and Letters.

Nikki Giovanni (1943–)

Yolande Cornelia Giovanni Jr. was born in Knoxville, Tennessee, but grew up in Cincinnati, Ohio. Giovanni is a world-renowned poet, writer, commentator, activist, and educator. She has written more than two dozen books, including volumes of poetry, illustrated children's books, and collections of essays. Her career of advocacy, creative writing, scholarship, and education has been recognized in part through her receipt of over twenty honorary doctorates; she has been recognized as well by national publications that have named her Woman of the Year. Giovanni has received governor's awards in the arts from both Tennessee and Virginia, and three volumes of her poetry—*Love Poems, Blues: For All the Changes,* and *Quilting the Black-Eyed Pea*—were winners of the NAACP Image Award. Since 1987 she has taught writing and literature at Virginia Technological University, where she is a University Distinguished Professor. *The Nikki Giovanni Poetry Collection* was a finalist for a 2003 Grammy Award in the category of spoken word.

Marita Golden (1950?–)

Marita Golden, a native of Washington, D.C., wrote as her first book *Migrations of the Heart* (1987), an autobiography that recounts her experience of marrying a Nigerian and living in Nigeria. She earned a bachelor's from American University and a master's degree from the Graduate School of Journalism at Columbia University. Golden is an author of both fiction and nonfiction, including *Long Distance Life* (1989), *Saving Our Sons* (1995), *The Edge of Heaven* (1997), *A Miracle Every Day* (1999), and *Don't Play in the Sun: One Woman's Journey through the Color Complex* (2004). She is the founder of the African American Writers Guild and of the Zora Neale Hurston/Richard Wright Foundation, which supports writers of African descent and offers an annual summer writer's workshop for black writers.

LANGSTON HUGHES (1902–1967)

Langston Hughes was born James Langston Hughes in Joplin, Missouri. His first published poem became his most famous, "The Negro Speaks of Rivers," and it appeared first in the *Brownie's Book*—a children's magazine published by the NAACP and the *Crisis*. One of Hughes's most well-known essays, "The Negro Artist and the Racial Mountain," appeared in the *Nation* in 1926 and later became an aesthetic manifesto of the Black Arts movement. In 1923, Hughes traveled abroad on a freighter to Senegal, Nigeria, Cameroon, Belgium Congo, Angola, and Guinea. He traveled as well in Europe and Russia. He finally made his home in Harlem and became one of the most prominent voices of the Harlem Renaissance. During that era, Hughes received a scholarship to Lincoln University, in Pennsylvania, and completed his bachelor's degree there in 1929. Later he was awarded Guggenheim and Rosenwald fellowships. Langston Hughes's prolific career as a writer included the publication of two novels, sixteen books of poems, collections of short stories and other fiction, editorial essays, three autobiographies, radio and television scripts and drama, and children's poetry. *Rivers,* a terrazzo and brass cosmogram by Houston Conwill, Esella Conwill Majozo, and Joseph DePace, and installed on the floor of the Schomburg Center for Research in Black Culture in Harlem, includes verses from Hughes's "The Negro Speaks of Rivers." Langston Hughes's ashes are buried there beneath the words "My soul has grown deep, like the rivers."

ZORA NEALE HURSTON (1891–1960)

Zora Neale Hurston was raised in the community that became the background for much of her writing, Eatonville, Florida—the first incorporated black township in the state. She received bachelor's degrees from Howard University and Barnard College of Columbia University. She rose to literary prominence in the years following the Harlem Renaissance, earning wide recognition as a novelist, folklorist, and anthropologist. Hurston moved from Washington, D.C., to New York City, which—despite many research trips to the Caribbean and the U.S. South—was to be her base during most of her literary career. She financed her endeavors with the help of literary patrons as well as awards from the Rosenwald and Guggenheim foundations. Her publications include *Jonah's Gourd Vine* (1934), an anthropological study of vodun, as well as *Mules and Men* (1935), *Moses, Man of the Mountain* (1939), and *Dust Tracks on a Road* (1942). Her final novel, *Seraph on the Suwanee,* appeared in 1948. In her later years Hurston was an essayist, writing conservatively and critically on racial politics.

JAMES WELDON JOHNSON (1871–1938)

James Weldon Johnson began his professional life as the principal of a primary school, and later of a high school, in the town of his birth, Jacksonville, Florida. He was founder of the *Daily American,* the first black daily newsletter, and was admitted to the Florida bar in 1897. Johnson and his brother

Rosamond composed the lyrics and music for "Lift Every Voice and Sing"—a piece internationally recognized as the "Negro national anthem." Johnson was a field secretary for the NAACP and also served as consul to Venezuela and Nicaragua during the Roosevelt and Taft administrations. He is remembered for his fiction and poetry, especially the sermons that make up *God's Trombones* (1927). The volume includes "The Creation" and "Go Down Death," works that became standard recitation performance pieces in black communities during the middle and later eras of the twentieth century. Johnson was the editor of *The Book of American Negro Poetry* (1922) and, with his brother Rosamond, *The Book of American Negro Spirituals* (1925). His autobiography, *Along This Way* (1933), is often read against his semifictional novel, *The Autobiography of an Ex-Colored Man* (1912). James Weldon Johnson held the Adam K. Spence Professor of Creative Literature chair at Fisk University until his death in 1938.

C. Eric Lincoln (1924–2000)

Charles Eric Lincoln was born in Athens, Alabama. At his death, he was the William Rand Kenan Jr. Professor Emeritus of Religion and Culture at Duke University. Lincoln, an ordained Methodist minister, was the author of more than twenty books, among them *The Black Muslims in America* (1961) and *The Black Church in the African-American Experience* with Lawrence Mamiya (1990), both of which were widely known and acclaimed. His publication of *The Black Muslims in America* occasioned Lincoln's close friendship with Malcolm X and became the standard text for understanding the Muslim movement in America. Lincoln, who taught at more than a dozen colleges and universities, was also the author of a novel, *The Avenue, Clayton City* (1988)—which received the Lillian Smith Award for Best Southern Fiction—and a collection of essays, *This Road since Freedom*. Lincoln was the founding president of the Black Academy of Arts and Letters and a fellow of the American Academy of Arts and Sciences.

Audre Lorde (1934–1992)

Audrey Geraldine Lorde, a graduate of Hunter College (B.A.) and Columbia University (M.L.S.), was born in New York City to parents who had immigrated to the United States from Grenada. She worked as a librarian in Mount Vernon and then New York City. After being turned down by other black colleges because she was a lesbian, including Talladega College, Lorde was granted a creative writing residency in 1968 at the historically black college Tougaloo, in Jackson, Mississippi. She later held the Thomas Hunter Chair of Literature at Hunter College. Lorde published six collections of prose and more than a dozen books of poetry. Her accomplishments were recognized by numerous awards and honors, including her designation, in 1991–1993, as New York State's poet laureate. She was cofounder of a press for African American women writers, the Kitchen Table: Women of Color Press, and was editor of the lesbian journal *Chrysalis*. In 1974, her third volume of poetry, *From a Land Where Other People Live,* was nominated for a National Book Award. This nomination brought her to national prominence and her next collections, *Coal* (1976) and *The Black Unicorn* (1978), received wide critical attention. Lorde is especially remembered for *The Cancer Journals* (1981) and a book of essays, *A Burst of Light* (1988), in which she recorded her fourteen-year battle with cancer. *The Cancer Journals* won the American Library Association's Gay Caucus Book of the Year Award. In 1982, Lorde published the classic *Zami: A New Spelling of My Name*—a "biomythography." Lorde died on November 17, 1992, in St. Croix. Her last poetry collection, *The Marvelous Arithmetics of Distance: Poems, 1987–1992*, was published posthumously in 1993.

MALCOLM X (1925–1965)

Malcolm X was born as Malcolm Little in Omaha, Nebraska, the son of a Baptist minister. In 1929 the Little family moved to Lansing, Michigan, in part because the family had been the target of harassment in Omaha. In Michigan, his father was killed by a streetcar, and his mother, traumatized by the loss of her husband, was institutionalized. Dropping out of school in the eighth grade, Malcolm Little went to New York to make a living, but he became involved in theft and was sentenced to a ten-year prison term on burglary charges in 1946, an incarceration that led to his conversion to membership in the Black Muslims. His public profile rose during the years following his release, and there was concern among the Muslims about his prominence. He was suspended from the Black Muslim movement by Elijah Muhammad after his public pronouncement that the assassination of U.S. president John Kennedy was an event that signified "the chickens came home to roost."

Malcolm X formed the Organization of Afro-American Unity and made a life-changing pilgrimage to Mecca, from which he returned with a new name, El-Hajj Malik El Shabazz, and a new focus on global brotherhood and justice. He had gained international prominence and a wide national audience before he was shot and killed at the Audubon Ballroom in Harlem in 1965. The men arrested for the shooting were members of the Nation of Islam.

PAULI MURRAY (1910–1985)

Anna Pauline Murray was born in Baltimore, Maryland, but her grandparents and her aunt raised her in Durham, North Carolina. She received a bachelor's degree from Hunter College, after which she worked for *Opportunity* magazine. In 1938 she tried to enter graduate school at the University of North Carolina at Chapel Hill but was denied admission because of her race. Murray attended law school at Howard University, was one of the founders of the Congress of Racial Equality in 1942, and attempted further study of law at Harvard University. This time she was denied entrance because she was a woman. She later received a master's in law from the University of California. Murray authored volumes in various fields, from *States' Laws on Race and Color* (1951) to a memoir titled *Proud Shoes: The Story of an American Family* (1956), to *Dark Testament* (1970), a book of poems. Murray studied at General Theological Seminary,

New York, and in 1977 became the first African American woman ordained to the priesthood of the Episcopal Church. Her autobiography, *Song in a Weary Throat: An American Pilgrimage* (1987), was published posthumously.

J. SAUNDERS REDDING (1906–1988)

Jay Saunders Redding was born in Wilmington, Delaware. He attended Lincoln University in Pennsylvania before he transferred to Brown University, where he received his bachelor's degree. After his graduation from Brown, he taught at Morehouse College in Atlanta but then returned to Brown for graduate study, earning his master's degree there in 1932. Redding's distinguished teaching career included positions at Southern University, Hampton Institute, and George Washington University. He also was a visiting professor at Brown, Grinnell College, and Duke University. His books include *On Being Negro in America* (1951) and *The Lonesome Road* (1958). His writing and teaching were informed by his teaching exchanges to India and to West Africa, and their excellence was recognized with the award of eight honorary degrees and a Rockefeller Foundation fellowship. He was twice awarded fellowships from the Guggenheim Foundation. Redding retired from Cornell University as the Ernest I. White Professor of American Studies and Humane Letters.

SONIA SANCHEZ (1934–)

Sonia Sanchez was born Wilsonia Benita Driver in Birmingham, Alabama. She moved to Harlem in the early 1940s and was awarded a bachelor's degree from Hunter College. Sanchez formed a writers' workshop in Greenwich Village, but eventually she moved to the West Coast and taught at San Francisco State University, where she instituted some of the first black studies courses in the nation. Sanchez is the author of plays, children's books, and more than a dozen books of poetry; she has been nominated for the NAACP Image and National Book Critics Circle awards. *Homegirls and Handgrenades* (1984) won an American Book Award from the Before Columbus Foundation. Her awards and honors include the Peace and Freedom Award from the Women's International League for Peace and Freedom, the Pennsylvania Governor's Award for Excellence in the Humanities, a National Endowment for the Arts award, and a Pew Fellowship in the Arts. She retired in 1999 from the faculty of Temple University, where she held the Laura Carnell chair in English.

RICHARD WRIGHT (1908–1960)

Richard Wright was born on a plantation near Natchez, Mississippi. The family moved to Memphis when Richard was six years old. For a time he was enrolled in a Seventh-Day Adventist school near Jackson, but he also attended a local public school for a few years. In 1924 the *Southern Register,* a local black newspaper, printed his first story, "The Voodoo of Hell's Half Acre." Wright moved to Chicago, where he worked as a post office clerk and became involved with the Communist Party and writing for their newspapers. His links to the

Communist Party continued after his move to New York in 1937, where he became the Harlem editor of the *Daily Worker*. His short story collection, *Uncle Tom's Children* (1938), was followed by the award of a Guggenheim fellowship. His first novel, *Native Son,* appeared in 1940. Wright moved to Paris in 1946, and the existentialism of that period is reflected in *The Outsider* (1953). *Savage Holiday* followed in 1954 and *The Long Dream* in 1958; another short story collection, *Eight Men,* was published posthumously in 1960. Wright authored two autobiographies: *Black Boy* (1945) and *American Hunger* (1977; published posthumously).

Notes

Prologue—A Reader's Place

1. Frederick Douglass, *Narrative of the Life of Frederick Douglass, an American Slave, Written by Himself* (1845; reprint, New York: Penguin Books, 1982), 35; subsequent reference, 80.

2. Louis Shores, "Library Service and the Negro," *Journal of Negro Education* 1, 3–4 (October 1932): 374–380.

1. Reading and Desire in a Room of Their Own

1. Jessie Fauset, "My House and a Glimpse of My Life Therein," *Crisis* 8 (July 1914): 143; subsequent references, 144, 145.

2. Marita Golden, *Migrations of the Heart* (New York: Doubleday, 1987), 10; subsequent references, 25, 222.

2. A Negro Library

1. W.E.B. Du Bois, "Books," in *Writings* (New York: Modern Library of America/Penguin, 1986), 1232; subsequent references, 1232–1234.

2. David Levering Lewis, *W.E.B. Du Bois: Biography of a Race, 1868–1919* (New York: Owl Books, 1994), 286.

3. Hazel Carby, *Race Men* (Cambridge: Harvard University Press, 2000), 10.

4. W.E.B. Du Bois, *The Souls of Black Folk* (1903; reprint, New York: Penguin, 1996), 90.

5. Angela Davis, *Angela Davis: An Autobiography* (1974; reprint, New York: International Publishers, 1974), 97; subsequent reference, 97.

6. Shores, "Library Service and the Negro," 376.

7. Municipal ordinance of Danville, Virginia, April 1960 (http://www.jimcrowhistory.org/geography/geography.htm).

8. Maurice Wheeler, "UNT Expert Says Brown v. Board of Education Altered the Foundation and Policies of Public Libraries," University of North Texas News Service, May 20, 2004.

9. Ralph Ellison, *Shadow and Act* (1964; reprint, New York: Vintage, 1995), 157–158.

10. Richard Wright, *Black Boy: American Hunger* (1945; reprint, New York: Perennial, 1993), 214; subsequent references, 214–220, 226.

3. On Censorship and Tarzan

1. John Hope Franklin, "A Life of Learning," in *Race and History: Selected Essays, 1938–1988* (Baton Rouge: Louisiana State University Press, 1990), 279–280.

2. Claudia Tate, ed., "Sonia Sanchez," in *Black Women Writers at Work* (New York: Continuum International Publishing Group, 1984), 146–147; subsequent reference, 147.

3. Pauli Murray, *Song in a Weary Throat* (New York: HarperCollins, 1987), 31.

4. Audre Lorde, *Zami, a New Spelling of My Name* (Freedom, CA: Crossing Press Feminist Series, 1983), 18–22.

5. Wilma Rudolph, *Wilma* (New York: Signet/New American Library, 1977), 15.

6. Carla Williams, "Reading Deeper: The Legacy of Dick and Jane in the Work of Clarissa Sligh," in *Image* 38, 3–4 (Fall/Winter 1995): 3.

4. A Prison Library

1. Megan Sweeney, "Racial House, Big House, Home: Contemporary Abolitionism in Toni Morrison's *Paradise*," *Meridians: Feminism, Race, Transnationalism* 4, 2 (2004): 40.

2. Eldridge Cleaver, *Soul on Ice* (1968; reprint, New York: Delta, 1999), 69; subsequent references, 70.

3. John Edgar Wideman, *Brothers and Keepers: A Memoir* (New York: Mariner Books, 2005), 229; subsequent reference, 87.

4. Alex Haley, *The Autobiography of Malcolm X (as Told to Alex Haley)* (1965; reprint, New York: Ballantine, 1992), 176; subsequent references, 176–180.

5. Claude Brown, *Manchild in the Promised Land* (1965; reprint, New York: Touchstone, 1999), 150.

6. Davis, *Autobiography,* 52; subsequent reference, 51.

5. The Anchor Bar

1. Susan Davis, "Entering the World through Language," in *Conversations with Rita Dove,* ed. Earl. G. Ingersoll, 38–52 (Jackson: University Press of Mississippi, 2003), 38.

2. Maya Angelou, *I Know Why the Caged Bird Sings* (New York: Random House, 1970), 14; subsequent references, 15, 100.

3. bell hooks, "Black Is a Woman's Color," *Callaloo* 12, 2 (Spring 1989): 384–385.

4. Davis, *Autobiography,* 97.

5. James Baldwin, *Notes of a Native Son* (Boston: Beacon Press, 1984), 5; subsequent references, 3–5.

6. A Proud Chestnut

1. James Weldon Johnson, *Along This Way* (1938; reprint, New York: Da Capo Press, 2000), 11; subsequent references, 96–98.

2. James Weldon Johnson, *Autobiography of an Ex-Colored* Man (1912; reprint, New York: Vintage, 1989), 121; subsequent references, 148. I am indebted to Rudolph Byrd for his helpful insights regarding Johnson's relationship with Dr. Summers.

3. Nikki Giovanni, *Gemini: An Extended Autobiographical Statement on My First Twenty-five Years of Being a Black Poet* (New York: Penguin, 1973), 141.

7. THE CHILDREN'S ROOM

1. Langston Hughes, *The Big Sea* (1940; reprint, New York: Hill and Wang, 1993), 95; subsequent references also 95.

2. Giovanni, *Gemini*, 140.

3. Murray, *Song in a Weary Throat*, 434; subsequent reference, 20.

8. MY MOTHER'S SINGING

1. Franklin, "A Life of Learning," 280.

2. Johnson, *Autobiography of an Ex-Colored Man*, 12.

3. C. Eric Lincoln, *Coming Through the Fire* (Durham, NC: Duke University Press, 2000), 57; subsequent references, 57–58, 156.

4. Ellison, *Shadow and Act*, 157; subsequent reference, 150.

5. Leon Forrest, *Relocations of the Spirit: Essays* (Wakefield, RI: Asphodel Press/Moyer Bell, 1994), 7.

9. READING RACE

1. John Grisham, *The Firm* (New York: Doubleday, 1991); subsequent reference, 376.

2. Emma Dunham Kelley-Hawkins, *Four Girls at Cottage City,* Schomburg Library of Nineteenth-Century American Writers, ed. Henry Louis Gates Jr. (1898; reprint, New York: Oxford University Press, 1988).

3. Henry Louis Gates Jr., *Colored People* (New York: Alfred A. Knopf, 1994), 95; subsequent references, 108–110, 16, 150, and 185.

4. Brown, *Manchild in the Promised Land,* 150.

5. Audre Lorde, "Uses of the Erotic," in *Sister Outsider: Essays and Speeches* (Trumansburg, NY: Crossing Press, 1984), 56.

6. Michael Eric Dyson, *Between God and Gangsta Rap* (New York: Oxford University Press, 1996), 16, 150.

10. THE CARD CATALOG

1. Zora Neale Hurston, *Dust Tracks on a Road* (Boston: J. B. Lippincott, 1942), 38–40; subsequent references, 98, 124, and 137.

2. J. Saunders Redding, *No Day of Triumph* (New York: Harper and Bros., 1942), 84.

3. Thomas Dixon, *The Leopard's Spots,* http://etext.lib.virginia.edu/toc/modeng/public/Dixleop.html.

4. Octavia Butler, "An Interview with Octavia Butler," in *Across the Wounded Galaxies: Interviews with Contemporary American Science Fiction Writers,* ed. Larry McCaffery, 54–70 (Urbana: University of Illinois Press, 1990), 60; subsequent references, 59.

5. S. Davis, "Entering the World through Language," 38.

6. Samuel Delany, *The Motion of Light in Water: Sex and Science Fiction Writing in the East Village, 1957–1965* (New York: Plume/New American Library, 1989), 10; subsequent references, 104.

7. Marilyn Johnson, "Oprah Winfrey: A Life in Books," *Life,* September 1997, 60.

8. Jamaica Kincaid, *A Small Place* (New York: Farrar, Straus and Giroux, 1988), 42.

Sources

Angelou, Maya. *I Know Why the Caged Bird Sings*. New York: Random House, 1970.

Baldwin, James. *Go Tell It on the Mountain*. 1953. Reprint. New York: Modern Library, 1995.

———. *Notes of a Native Son*. Boston: Beacon Press, 1984.

Brown, Claude. *Manchild in the Promised Land*. 1965. Reprint. New York: Touchstone, 1999.

Butler, Octavia. "An Interview with Octavia Butler." In *Across the Wounded Galaxies: Interviews with Contemporary American Science Fiction Writers*, ed. Larry McCaffery, 54–70. Urbana: University of Illinois Press, 1990.

Carby, Hazel. *Race Men*. Cambridge: Harvard University Press, 2000.

Carroll, Charles. *The Negro, a Beast, or, In the Image of God*. St. Louis: American Book and Bible House, 1900.

Cleaver, Eldridge. *Soul on Ice*. 1968. Reprint. New York: Delta, 1999.

Davis, Angela. *Angela Davis: An Autobiography*. 1974. Reprint. New York: International Publishers, 1988.

Davis, Susan. "Entering the World through Language." In *Conversations with Rita Dove*, ed. Earl. G. Ingersoll, 38–52. Jackson: University Press of Mississippi, 2003.

Delany, Samuel. *The Motion of Light in Water: Sex and Science Fiction Writing in the East Village, 1957–1965*. New York: Plume/New American Library, 1989.

Dixon, Thomas. *The Leopard's Spots*. http://etext.lib.virginia.edu/toc/modeng/public/DixLeap.html.

Douglass, Frederick. *Narrative of the Life of Frederick Douglass, an American Slave, Written by Himself*. 1845. Reprint. New York: Penguin, 1982.

Du Bois, W.E.B. "Books." In *Writings*. New York: Modern Library of America/Penguin, 1986.

———. *The Souls of Black Folk*. 1903. Reprint. New York: Penguin, 1996.

Dyson, Michael Eric. *Between God and Gangsta Rap*. New York: Oxford University Press, 1996.

———. "Shakespeare and Smokey Robinson." *New York Times Book Review*, 19 November 1995, 47.

Ellison, Ralph. *Shadow and Act*. 1964. Reprint. New York: Vintage, 1995.

Fauset, Jessie. "My House and a Glimpse of My Life Therein." *Crisis* 8 (July 1914): 143–145.

Forrest, Leon. *Relocations of the Spirit: Essays*. Wakefield, RI: Asphodel Press/Moyer Bell, 1994.

Franklin, John Hope. "A Life of Learning." In *Race and History: Selected Essays, 1938–1988*. Baton Rouge: Louisiana State University Press, 1990.

Gates, Henry Louis, Jr. *Colored People*. New York: Alfred A. Knopf, 1994.

————. *The Signifying Monkey: A Theory of African-American Literary Criticism.* New York: Oxford University Press, 1988.

Giovanni, Nikki. *Gemini: An Extended Autobiographical Statement on My First Twenty-five Years of Being a Black Poet.* New York: Penguin, 1973.

————. *Racism 101.* North Yorkshire, UK: Quill, 1995.

Golden, Marita. *Migrations of the Heart.* Reprint. New York: Doubleday, 1987.

Grisham, John. *The Firm.* New York: Doubleday, 1991.

Haley, Alex. *The Autobiography of Malcolm X (as Told to Alex Haley).* 1965. Reprint. New York: Ballantine, 1992.

Heath, Shirley Brice. "Toward an Ethnohistory of Writing in American Education." In *Writing: The Nature, Development, and Teaching of Written Communication,* ed. Marcia Farr Whiteman, 25–45. Hillsdale, NJ: Lawrence Erlbaum Associates, 1981.

Herder, Dale M. "Haldeman-Julius, the Little Blue Books and the Theory of Popular Culture." *Journal of Popular Culture* 4, 4 (Spring 1971): 881–891.

Hooks, Bell. "Black Is a Woman's Color." *Callaloo* 12, 2 (Spring 1989): 382–388.

Hughes, Langston. *The Big Sea.* 1940. Reprint. New York: Hill and Wang, 1993.

Hurston, Zora Neale. *Dust Tracks on a Road.* Boston: J. B. Lippincott, 1942.

————. *Seraph on the Suwannee.* 1948. Reprint. New York: Harper Perennial, 1991.

Ingersoll, Earl G., ed. *Conversations with Rita Dove.* Jackson: University Press of Mississippi, 2003.

Johnson, James Weldon. *Along This Way.* 1938. Reprint. New York: Da Capo Press, 2000.

————. *Autobiography of an Ex-Colored Man.* 1912. Reprint. New York: Vintage, 1989.

Johnson, Marilyn. "Oprah Winfrey: A Life in Books." *Life Magazine,* September 1997, 44–60.

Kelley-Hawkins, Emma Dunham. *Four Girls at Cottage City.* 1898. Schomburg Library of Nineteenth-Century Black American Writers, ed. Henry Louis Gates Jr. New York: Oxford University Press, 1988.

Kincaid, Jamaica. *A Small Place.* New York: Farrar, Straus and Giroux, 1988.

Lewis, David Levering. *W.E.B. Du Bois: Biography of a Race, 1868–1919.* New York: Owl Books, 1994.

Lincoln, C. Eric. *Coming Through the Fire.* Durham, NC: Duke University Press, 2000.

Lorde, Audre. "Uses of the Erotic." In *Sister Outsider: Essays and Speeches.* Trumansburg, NY: Crossing Press, 1984.

————. *Zami, a New Spelling of My Name.* Freedom, CA: Crossing Press, 1983.

Mencken, H. L. *The Book of Prefaces.* 1917. Reprint. Kila, MT: Kessinger Publishing, 2005.

Morrison, Toni. *The Bluest Eye.* 1970. Reprint. New York: Alfred A. Knopf, 1993.

————. *Jazz.* New York: Alfred A. Knopf, 1992.

Municipal ordinance of Danville, Virginia. April 1960 (http://www.jimcrow history.org/geography/geography.htm).

Murray, Pauli. *Song in a Weary Throat*. New York: HarperCollins, 1987.

Redding, J. Saunders. *No Day of Triumph*. New York: Harper and Bros., 1942.

Rudolph, Wilma. *Wilma*. New York: Signet/New American Library, 1977.

Shores, Louis. "Library Service and the Negro." *Journal of Negro Education* 1, 3–4 (October 1932): 374–380.

Sweeney, Megan. "Racial House, Big House, Home: Contemporary Abolitionism in Toni Morrison's *Paradise*." *Meridians: Feminism, Race, Transnationalism* 4, 2 (2004): 40–67.

Tate, Claudia, ed. "Sonia Sanchez." In *Black Women Writers at Work*. New York: Continuum International Publishing Group, 1984.

Wheeler, Maurice. *Unfinished Business: Race, Equity and Diversity in Library and Information Science Education*. Lanham, MD: Scarecrow Press/Rowman and Littlefield, 2004.

Wideman, John Edgar. *Brothers and Keepers: A Memoir*. New York: Mariner Books, 2005.

Williams, Carla. "Reading Deeper: The Legacy of Dick and Jane in the Work of Clarissa Sligh." *Image* 38, 3–4 (Fall/Winter 1995).

Wright, Richard. *Black Boy: American Hunger*. 1945. Reprint. New York: Perennial, 1993.

Index

activism, 125. *See also* civil rights movement; politics
African Methodist Episcopal Church, 57, 132
alcohol, 93–94
Alexander, Margaret Walker, 157
American Mercury (magazine), 34
Amistad mural (Woodruff), 186–190
Anchor Bar (Buffalo, NY), 93–94, 102–103
Andersen, Hans Christian, 129, 171
Anderson, Marian, 158
Angelou, Maya, 95–100, 195; *I Know Why the Caged Bird Sings*, 95–96, 158
Annals of the American Academy: "The American Negro," 36
Annunzio, Gabrielle d': *The Flame of Life*, 124
anthologies, 59, 61, 63–64, 73. *See also Columbian Orator;* textbooks
Antigua, 187
Armstrong, Louis, 158
attic metaphor, 18–19, 21–22, 24. *See also* Fauset, Jessie Redmond
audience, 178, 179, 182, 184, 185
Audubon Regional Library (Clinton, LA), 41–42
authors, 176; "high-brow," 185; race of, 148–150; self and, 186. *See also specific authors;* writing
autonomy, 155–156

Baker, Augusta, 66–67
Baldwin, James, 101–102, 139, 195; "Autobiographical Notes," 102; *Go Tell It on the Mountain*, 78, 148; *Notes of a Native Son*, 102, 155
Balzac, Honoré de: *Droll Stories*, 111–112

Barrie, J. M.: *Sentimental Tommy*, 178
beauty, 109–110
"Behold That Star!" (spiritual), 132
Beowulf, 100
Bethune, Mary McLeod, 152
Bible, 101–102; Hurston and, 171–173, 175. *See also* Christianity; religion
Birmingham (AL) Public Library, 40
black arts movement, 22–23, 123
Black Muslim movement, 86
blue books (Haldeman-Julius), 35, 44, 175, 179
Blume, Judy, 107
Boccacio, Giovanni: *Decameron*, 111–112
book clubs, 184–185
bookmarks, 9, 24, 79, 81, 125, 180; significance of, 52–53
bookmobiles, 41. *See also* libraries
books, as personal or cultural markers, 6–7, 32, 119, 151, 162–163, 168, 181, 193; Angelou and, 95, 96, 98, 103; Cleaver and, 79, 81; Davis and, 84, 100; Dyson and, 158, 160; Fauset and, 20; Gates and, 151, 154–155; Golden and, 22, 23; Hughes and, 122; Hurston and, 175; Johnson and, 113; Lincoln and, 138; Lorde and, 67; Malcolm X and, 81, 86; Murray and, 126, 128; and public libraries, 40, 44–45; Redding and, 177, 178, 179; Washington and, 176; Winfrey and, 185–186; Wright and, 49–50, 51
Bradley, Marion Zimmer: Darkover series, 183
Brooks, Gwendolyn, 22, 23, 59, 63–64, 71, 123; "Annie Allen," 123

Brothers Grimm, 109, 129

Brown, Claude: *Manchild in the Promised Land,* 83–84, 152

Brown, Louise, 41

Brown, Quincy, 41–42

Browning, Elizabeth: *Aurora Leigh,* 19

Brown v. Board of Education (1954), 42, 63, 69

Brown v. Louisiana (1966), 42, 45

Buffalo (NY) Public Library, 120, 129

Burroughs, Edgar Rice: *Tarzan,* 58–59, 70–71

Butler, Octavia, 128, 181–184, 195–196

Butler, Samuel: *The Way of All Flesh,* 124

Card, Orson Scott: *Ender's Game,* 77, 88

card catalogs, 169, 190–191

Carnegie, Andrew, philanthropy of, 45

Carnes, Paul, 57

Carr, Julian S., 127

Carroll, Charles: *The Negro, a Beast, or, In the Image of God,* 176–177

Cash, W. G.: *The Mind of the South,* 137–138

Catholics, 45, 47

censorship, 70–71, 76, 81, 110, 111–114

character, 28, 31

characters, 144–146, 148; portrayals of, 176–179

children, 69, 176; libraries and, 118–119, 128–129; literature of, 178; reading for, 106–110, 115–116. *See also* Holloway, Ayana; Holloway, Bem

Christianity, 172. *See also* Bible; Catholics; religion

civil rights movement, 22–23, 41, 125. *See also* politics

Clapp, Ouida Harrison (mother), 56–59, 61, 69–73, 132–134, 140–141; Grisham and, 144–145, 164–165; lemon meringue pie, 71–73; letters of, 56–59, 61

Clark, Kenneth Bancroft, 69

Clark, Mamie Phipps, 69

Cleaver, Eldridge, 78–79, 81, 83, 196; *Soul on Ice,* 78

Clinton, Bill, 28

Clinton, Louisiana, 41

Columbian Orator, The (anthology), 7–8

comic books, 92–93, 103, 179, 182, 184

Communism, 85

composers, 136. *See also* music

conduct, 6, 28–30, 163

Conrad, Joseph: *Heart of Darkness,* 124

consciousness, 161. *See also* mind

Cooper, Anna Julia, 38, 58; "The Negro as Presented in American Literature," 177; *A View from the South,* 55; "A Voice from the South," 27

Cossitt Library (Memphis, TN), 46

Crisis (magazine), 16, 19–21, 34–35, 126; libraries and, 33, 36–39

culture, 38–39, 100, 114–115; education and, 61–64; libraries and, 63–67; literacy and, 180; race and, 156, 158, 162; tradition and, 57–59. *See also* education; libraries; literature; music; reading; tradition

Danville, Virginia, 42

Davis, Angela, 42–43, 84–85, 100, 196–197

death, 192–193

Delaney, Samuel, 181, 183–184, 197; *The Motion of Light in Winter,* 143

Depression era, 33

De Quincey, Thomas: *Confessions of an English Opium Eater,* 175

desire, 17, 21, 24–25, 68, 88–89; and Angelou, 95, 96–97; and displacement, 19; and hooks, 98; and Johnson, 114; and text, 8

Dick and Jane readers, 68–69

Dickens, Charles, 179; *David Copperfield,* 108; *A Tale of Two Cities,* 99–102, 151

Dickinson, Emily, 99

displacement, 16, 19, 81, 83

Dixon, Thomas, 176–177; *The Birth of a Nation,* 176; *The Leopard's Spots,* 176

"doll test," 69–71

Dostoevsky, Fyodor, 162

Douglass, Frederick, 20, 51; *Columbian Orator* and, 7–8; *Narrative of the Life of,* 7–8, 99

Dove, Rita, 92–93, 167, 182, 197

Dreiser, Theodore: *Jennie Gerhardt,* 50; *Sister Carrie,* 50

Du Bois, W.E.B., 21, 100, 162, 197–198; *Autobiography of,* 84; "On the Training of Black Men," 38; *The Souls of Black Folk,* 12, 38, 39, 86

Duke University, 28–29

Dunbar, Paul Lawrence, 62, 95, 178, 179; Hughes and, 120; *Works,* 62

Durant, Will: *Story of Civilization,* 86, 87

Dyson, Michael Eric, 156–160, 178, 198; *Between God and Gangsta Rap: Bearing Witness to Black Culture,* 156; intellect and, 157, 159, 161–162

Ebony (magazine), 3–5

eclecticism, 179–180

economic challenges, 33–34

education, 2–7, 38; culture and, 61–64; curriculum, 124, 175; Dick and Jane readers, 68–69; formal type of, 87; New England and, 138; politics and, 85; religion and, 58–59; whites and, 178. *See also* culture; libraries; literature; reading

Eliot, T. S., 123, 183

Ellison, Ralph, 138–139; *Invisible Man,* 44; *Shadow and Act,* 44

enunciation, 69–70

epistle form, 24, 59

erotica, 111–112, 154. *See also* censorship

Europe, 137, 158, 161

European writers, 39

fairy tales, 106, 118, 129, 178

family, death and, 192–193. *See also* children; Clapp, Ouida Harrison; father; Holloway, Ayana; Holloway, Bem; mother; parents

father, 92–94, 103. *See also* family; parents

Faulkner, William, 139

Fauset, Jessie Redmon, 16–24, 37–38, 198; attic metaphor and, 18–19, 21–22; "My House and a Glimpse of My Life Therein," 16–17, 19–21

feminism, 23, 125. *See also* women

fiction, 24–25, 92–94. *See also* literature; novels; stories

First Amendment, 42, 111

First Congress of Colored Women (1895), 177–178

Fisk University, 10; Jubilee Singers and, 137–138. *See also* Shores, Louis

Flaubert, Gustave: *Madame Bovary,* 22–23

Flynn, Elizabeth Gurley, 85

Folsom State Prison, 78, 80

Forrest, Leon, 199; "At Home in the Windy City," 139

Fosdick, Harry Emerson, 56–57
Franklin, John Hope, 61, 134, 199
free speech, 42

Gandhi, Mohandas K., 87
Gates, Henry Louis, Jr., 28–29, 111, 148, 150, 151–155, 157, 163, 199–200; *Colored People*, 150; *The Signifying Monkey*, 151–152
gender, 19, 23, 125, 154
Gibson, John: *The Remarkable Advancement*, 125
Gilmore v. Lynch (1971), 80
Giovanni, Nikki, 114–115, 200; *Gemini*, 123; *Quilting the Black-Eyed Pea*, 131
Golden, Marita, 21–24, 154–155, 200; *Migrations of the Heart*, 21–24
Gollumb, Joseph: *Albert Schweitzer: Genius in the Jungle*, 151–153
Gray, Thomas: "Elegy Written in a Country Churchyard," 160, 174
"Great Is Thy Faithfulness" (spiritual), 132
Greenville, South Carolina, 42–43
Grey, Zane: *Riders of the Purple Sage*, 122
Griffith, D. W.: *The Birth of a Nation* (film), 177
Grimm Brothers, 109, 129
Grisham, John, 144–146, 164–165; *The Firm*, 144, 165; *The Painted House*, 164

Haldeman-Julius, Emanuel, 35; blue books of, 44
Haley, Alex: *Autobiography of Malcolm X*, 81–83, 85–86
Harlem, New York, 152, 192; New York Public Library, Harlem branch, 64–67. *See also* Schomburg Library
Harlem Renaissance, 136–137
Harrison, Frank, 132–133

Harvard Classics, 138, 159–160, 179
Hayes, Roland, 158
Hearn, Lafcadio, 19
Heaven Bound (folk drama), 133
Heinlein, Robert: "Gulf," 184
Henderson, Zenna: *Pilgrimage*, 182–183
Herbert, Frank: *Dune*, 183
Hercules, 171
Herodotus, 87
hierarchies, 96
"high-brow," 185
hip-hop, 157, 159
history, 123, 186, 187
Hoffman, Linda, 151–153
Holliday, Billie, 131
Holloway, Ayana (daughter), 14–16, 24–25, 28–30, 52, 77, 106–107, 115–116, 192–193
Holloway, Bem (son), 28–30, 70, 77, 192–193; death of, 51–53; prison and, 88–89
home, reading at, 3–6
hooks, bell, 98–99
Howard University, 175–176
Hughes, Langston, 59, 62, 63–64, 201; autobiographies of, 119, 122–124; *The Big Sea*, 119; "Dream Variation," 117; "The Negro Mother," 61; "A Negro Speaks of Rivers," 61
Hurst, Fannie, 170; *Imitation of Life*, 170
Hurston, Zora Neale, 173–176, 179, 201; *Dust Tracks on a Road*, 170, 173, 176; myths and, 170–172, 175; *Seraph on the Suwanee*, 148–149; whites and, 169–170
hymns, 132–133. *See also* music; spirituals

images, 67–68, 151
"In Bright Mansions" (spiritual), 132
individualism, 39

influence, 102

integration, 62–63, 63, 69

intellect, 34, 38, 111, 113, 126; race and, 150, 157, 159, 161–162. *See also* education; mind

intimacy, 7–8, 17, 21, 24, 53, 89, 97

Irish, 45

Islam, 86

Jackson, George: *Soledad Brother*, 85

Jackson, Mahalia, 158

"Jerusalem" (spiritual), 132

Jim Crow laws, 10, 44, 45, 149

Johnson, James Weldon, 62, 108, 151, 153–154, 179, 201–202; *Along This Way*, 103, 107, 109, 111–113; *Autobiography of an Ex-Colored Man*, 110–112, 134; "The Creation," 61, 70, 97–98, 100, 103; "Go Down Death," 103; *God's Trombones*, 61, 139; *Seven Negro Sermons in Verse*, 103

Jones, Claudia, 85

Joplin, Scott, 158

Journal of Negro Education, 40

Jubilee Singers, 137–138

judgment, 28, 30–31. *See also* conduct

Kallen, Homer, 57

Keats, John: "Ode to a Nightingale," 110

Kelley-Hawkins, Emma Dunham, 148–150, 163; *Four Girls at Cottage City*, 148

Kenan, Randall: *Let the Dead Bury the Dead*, 105

Kincaid, Jamaica: *A Small Place*, 187

King, Martin Luther, Jr., 160

Kipling, Rudyard, 171; *Plain Tales from the Hills*, 173

Ku Klux Klan, 177

Lama, Victor, 2

Lang, Andrew, 106, 118

language, 69–70, 102, 167

Larsen, Nella, 38

Lee, Don (Haki Madhubuti), 22, 23

Le Guin, Ursula K.: *The Dispossessed*, 183

letter form, 24

Lewis, David Levering, 33

Lewis, Sinclair: *Main Street*, 50

Liberal Religious Youth (LRY), 57

libraries, 10–11, 30–32, 84–85, 101, 103; branch service, 40–41; in Buffalo, NY, 93–94; children and, 118–119, 128–129; *Crisis* and, 33, 36–39; culture and, 63–67; in Durham, NC, 126–128; Hurston and, 168–170; prison, 79–83, 87–88; public use of, 39–41, 43, 46, 120–121; Savery Library, 186–190; segregation and, 40–42, 44–45; shelving books at, 168–169, 192–193; stories and, 14–16, 24; Wright and, 45, 47–51. *See also* culture; education; literature; reading; *individual libraries*

Life (magazine), 185

Lincoln, C. Eric, 134–137, 158, 202; *Coming Through the Fire: Surviving Race and Place in America*, 134, 162

literacy, 9, 11, 81, 100; culture and, 180

literature, 35, 71, 78; children and, 178; Negro libraries and, 36–37; tradition and, 61–65, 101; world, 87. *See also* culture; reading

Longfellow, Henry Wadsworth: *Hiawatha*, 120

Lorde, Audre, 66–67, 69, 202–203; "Black Mother Woman," 91; *Sister Outsider*, 154; "Uses of the Erotic," 154; *Zami*, 67

Lover, Samuel: *Handy Andy: An Irish Tale*, 108

Madhubuti, Haki. *See* Lee, Don
magazines, 3–5, 11, 34–35, 126
Mailer, Norman: *An American Dream,*
    78–79
Malcolm X, 92, 135, 203; *Autobiog-
    raphy of,* 81–83, 85–86
Mason, Charlotte, 170
Matthews, Victoria Earle: "The
    Value of Race Literature," 177–
    178
Maupassant, Guy de, 122
Mecca, 87
Medallion textbook series, 59–61,
    70–71, 73
memories, 67–68
memorization, 97. *See also* recitation
memory, 32, 52–53. *See also* tradition
Memphis, Tennessee, 45, 50, 129
Mencken, H. L., 47–49; *A Book of
    Prefaces,* 49–50
Mendel, Gregor: *Findings in Genetics,*
    86
Millay, Edna St. Vincent: "Renas-
    cence," 99
Milton, John: *Paradise Lost,* 173
mind, 137–138. *See also* intellect
ministry, 125, 128
Modern Library (publisher), 35
Morrison, Toni: *Beloved,* 191; *The
    Bluest Eye,* 68; *Jazz,* 1, 7, 8, 24;
    Paradise, 76; *Tar Baby,* 148
Mosley, Walter, 28
mother, 69–73, 132–134, 140–141;
    and Grisham, 144–145, 164–165;
    letters of, 56–59, 61
Motown, 159
Muhammad, Elijah, 86
multiculturalism, 59, 156. *See also*
    culture
Murray, Pauli, 125–126, 128, 203–
    204; *Song in a Weary Throat,* 62
music, 131–134, 136–139, 158–159;
    text and, 140–141

Muslims, 86
myths, Hurston and, 170–172, 175

NAACP (National Association for
    the Advancement of Colored
    People), 16, 33, 41, 126
National Geographic (magazine), 3, 5
National Organization for Women
    (NOW), 125
Nation (magazine), 34
naturalism, 50
Negro problem, Baldwin on, 101
New England, 138
newspapers, 34–35
nonfiction, 92
Norfolk (MA) Prison Colony, 82, 135
Norse myths, 170–171
North, 40, 42, 63, 135–138, 178, 190
North Carolina prisons, 76
novels, 22, 23, 50, 144–145. *See also*
    fiction; stories

Olmsted, Frederick Law, 87
Oprah's Book Club, 184–185
oral traditions, 138–139, 178
oratory, 107
ownership, 20

Palmer Memorial Institute, 31
parents, 92–93, 100, 103, 107–111,
    112–114. *See also* children; family;
    father; mother
Parker, Charlie, 131
Parkhurst collection, 82–83, 87, 158
passing, 147, 170
Peter and His Pony (children's book),
    109
place, 9–12. *See also* displacement
Plessy v. Ferguson (1896), 41, 44
poetry, 62, 123, 160
politics, 10; civil rights and, 22; civil
    rights movement and, 125; educa-
    tion and, 85; gender and, 23; race

and, 4–5; reading and, 158–159; women and, 38

pornography, 111. *See also* censorship

Pound, Ezra, 123

prison, 76–78, 84–85, 135, 152; libraries and, 79–83, 87–88

privilege, 135–136

protest, 41–42. *See also* activism; civil rights movement

public: presentation, 88, 179; reading, 184–186

Pushkin, Alexander, 63

quotation, 105, 159

race, 7, 11–12, 20, 115; absence of, 180–181; Dyson and, 156–160; Gates and, 151–155; Grisham and, 144–146, 164–165; intellect and, 157, 159, 161–162; Kelley-Hawkins and, 148–150; offensive portrayals of, 176–179; politics and, 4–5; reading and, 94–99, 143–148; representation and, 58–59, 144–150, 152, 163–164

reading, 7–8, 102; children and, 106–110, 115–116; Dyson and, 156–160; Gates and, 151–155; Grisham and, 144–146, 164–165; habits, 45; home and, 3–6; intellect and, 157, 159, 161–162; Kelley-Hawkins and, 148–150; place and, 9–12; public, 184–186; race and, 94–99, 143–148. *See also* culture; education; libraries; literature; *specific authors*

realism, 50

recitation, 61, 70, 97–98, 100

Redding, J. Saunders, 177–178, 204; *No Day of Triumph,* 13, 176

religion, 56–58, 101–102. *See also* Bible; Christianity

representation, 30–31, 58–59, 124, 134

Republicans, 158

responsibility, 30. *See also* conduct

Robeson, Paul, 158

Rogers, J. A., 86

Romanticism, 98–99

Rossner, Judith: *Attachments,* 22–23

Roth v. United States (1957), 111

Rudolph, Wilma, 68

Sanchez, Sonia, 62–64, 204

sanctuary, 77, 88

Santayana, George, 56

Sartre, Jean-Paul: *Les Mots,* 161

Savery Library (Talladega College), 186–187, 190; *Amistad* mural in, 188–189

Schomburg Library (Harlem, New York, NY), 64–67

school, public, 59, 69. *See also* education

Schweitzer, Albert, 151–152

science fiction, 181–184

Scopes trial (1925), and Wright, 47–49

Scott, Walter, 108; *Tales of a Grandfather,* 110–111

Scott Foresman, Inc. (textbook company), 56, 58–59, 61, 68–70, 73

segregation, 62–63; libraries and, 40–42, 44–45; psychological effects of, 69. *See also* Wright, Richard: libraries and

self-authorship, 186

Sendak, Maurice: *Where the Wild Things Are,* 89

"separate but equal," 41–42

sermons, 102, 139–140, 178

Shakespeare, William, 95–98, 162, 176; *The Merchant of Venice,* 97–98; *Romeo and Juliet,* 70–71; sonnet 29, 96–97

Shaw, Solomon: *Dying Testimonies,* 126, 128
Shores, Louis, 10, 41, 44; "Library Service and the Negro," 40
Silk, Miss (librarian), 118–119
sixties era, 4, 23. *See also* civil rights movement
slavery, 8, 62–63; *Amistad* mural and, 186–190; histories of, 86
Smith, Bessie, 158
Snow, Edgar, 84
song. *See* music
Songs of Zion (songbook), 140
South, 40, 42, 63, 135–138, 178, 190
speech, 102
spirituals, 131–132. *See also* hymns; music
stereotypes, 31, 51, 69–71, 146, 162
Stevenson, Robert Louis, 171
Stoddard, John: *Lectures,* 126
Stone, Irving: *The Agony and the Ecstasy,* 153–154
stories, 14–16, 24–25. *See also* fiction; novels
Stowe, Harriet Beecher: *Uncle Tom's Cabin,* 87, 92, 101, 176
Supreme Court, U.S., 63, 69, 80

Talladega College, 56–57, 186–187, 190; choir of, 132–133
Tarzan, see Burroughs, Edgar Rice
Taylor, Holly, 149
Tennyson, Alfred: "Ulysses," 159
text, music and, 133, 138, 140–141
textbooks, 56, 58–59, 61, 71
texts, common, 179–180
theology, 110
Time (magazine), 3
Topeka, Kansas, 119, 121
tradition, 81, 95–100; culture and, 57–59, 114–115; literature and, 61–65, 101; music and, 133–134; oral, 97–98, 178; recitation and,

70. *See also* culture; libraries; literature; memory; music; religion
transformation, 82, 85
travel narratives, 118
"Trial of the Captives," *see Amistad* mural
Trinity School, 135–136
Turner, Nat, 87
"Twelve Gates to the City" (spiritual), 132

Unitarian Universalist church, 57, 58, 132
urban violence, 161

values, 56
violence, 161

Walker, Alice, 148
Ward, Mary: *Robert Elsmere,* 19
Washington, Booker T., 176; *The Story of the Negro,* 41; *Up from Slavery,* 101
weeklies, 34–35. *See also* magazines; newspapers
Wells, Ida B., 58
White, Walter, 33. *See also* NAACP
whiteness, 67, 147–148; authors and, 100; civilization and, 59; tradition and, 96–97, 99–100; writers and, 64
whites, 145, 153; as audience, 9, 178–179, 182, 184; as characters, 144–146, 148; children and, 69; Hurston and, 169–170; minds of, 137–138
Whitman, Walt: "O Captain, My Captain," 99
Wideman, John Edgar, 81, 83
Wilder, Thornton: *Our Town,* 133
Willard, Nancy, 52
Williams, Robert F.: *Negroes with Guns,* 79

Wilson, Augusta Jane: *Vashti—Or Until Death Do Us Part,* 110–111

Winfrey, Oprah, 184–185

women, 23, 25; libraries and, 38; prison and, 84–85; stereotypes of, 20. *See also* feminism

Wonder, Stevie, 158

Wonders of the World (book series), 86

Woodruff, Hale, 187–188; *Amistad* mural, 186, 189–190

Woodson, Carter G.: *Negro History,* 86

Wright, Richard, 129, 136–137, 204–205; *Black Boy,* 45, 51, 114–115; libraries and, 45, 47–51

writing, 50; tradition and, 101–102. *See also* authors; characters

Yerby, Frank, 148, 149

About the Author

Karla FC Holloway is the William R. Kenan Jr. Professor of English, Law, and Women's Studies at Duke University, where she teaches courses in literature, law, and biocultural studies. Among her books are *Passed On: African American Mourning Stories—A Memorial* and *Codes of Conduct: Race, Ethics, and the Color of Our Character*.